JEHOVAH-JIREH: A TREATISE ON PROVIDENCE

JEHOVAH-JIREH: A TREATISE ON PROVIDENCE

By

William S. Plumer

This book was written in the prevailing style of that period. Language and spelling have been left original in an effort to give the full flavor of this classic work.

Bottom of the Hill Publishing

Memphis, TN

www.BottomoftheHillPublishing.com

ISBN: 978-1-61203-689-2

Abraham named the place "Jehovah-jireh." (The Lord Will Provide) This name has now become a proverb: "On the mountain of the Lord it will be provided." *Genesis 22:14*

I would assert eternal Providence,
And justify the ways of God to men.

"Our God is in heaven and does whatever He pleases!" *Psalm 115:3*

"For I know that the Lord is great; our Lord is greater than all gods. The Lord does whatever He pleases in heaven and on earth, in the seas and all the depths!" *Psalm 135:5-6*

"Hallelujah! For the Lord our God, the Almighty, reigns!" *Revelation 19:6*

Content

"I know that You can do all things; no plan of Yours can be thwarted." Job 42:2

"My purpose will stand, and I will do all that I please. What I have said, that will I bring about; what I have planned, that will I do." Isaiah 46:10-11

"The plan of Him who works out everything in conformity with the purpose of His will." Ephesians 1:11

"This is the plan determined for the whole world." Isaiah 14:26

PROVIDENCE ASSERTED

Therefore I tell you, do not worry about your life, what you will eat or drink; or about your body, what you will wear. Is not life more important than food, and the body more important than clothes? Look at the birds of the air; they do not sow or reap or store away in barns, and yet your heavenly Father feeds them. Are you not much more valuable than they? Who of you by worrying can add a single hour to his life? And why do you worry about clothes? See how the lilies of the field grow. They do not labor or spin. Yet I tell you that not even Solomon in all his splendor was dressed like one of these. If that is how God clothes the grass of the field, which is here today and tomorrow is thrown into the fire, will he not much more clothe you, O you of little faith? (Jesus) Matt. 6:26-30

The life of every living thing is in His hand, as well as the breath of all mankind. (Job) 12:10

God sent me ahead of you to establish you as a remnant within the land and to keep you alive by a great deliverance. Therefore it was not you who sent me here, but God. (Joseph) Gen 45:7-8

As your days, so shall your strength be. (Moses) Deut 33:25

The Lord is King forever and ever. (David) Psalm 10:16

O Lord Almighty, God of Israel—you are the God, even you alone, of all the kingdoms of the earth. (Hezekiah)

Do you not know? Have you not heard? Has it not been told you from the beginning? Have you not understood since the earth was founded? He sits enthroned above the circle of the earth, and its people are like grasshoppers. He stretches out the heavens like a canopy, and spreads them out like a tent to live in. He brings princes to naught and reduces the rulers of this world to nothing. No sooner are they planted, no sooner are they sown, no sooner do they take root in the ground, than he blows on them and they wither, and a whirlwind sweeps them away like chaff. (Isaiah)

But the Lord is the true God; he is the living God, the eternal King. When he is angry, the earth trembles; the nations cannot endure his wrath. . . . O Lord, I know that the way of man is not in himself. (Jeremiah.)

In him we live and move and have our being. (Paul)

Now listen, you who say, "Today or tomorrow we will go to this or that city, spend a year there, carry on business and make money." Why, you do not even know what will happen tomorrow. What is your life? You are a mist that appears for a little while and then vanishes. Instead, you ought to say, "If it is the Lord's will, we will live and do this or that." (James)

The Lord knows how to deliver the godly out of temptation, and to reserve the unjust unto the day of judgment to be punished. (Peter)

Then I heard again what sounded like the shout of a huge crowd, or the roar of mighty ocean waves, or the crash of loud thunder: "Hallelujah! For the Lord our God, the Almighty, reigns!"

He who rules the raging of the sea, knows also how to check the designs of the ungodly. I submit myself with reverence to his Holy will. (Racine)

God's power as well as his wisdom gives him a right to govern the world—nothing can equal him, therefore nothing can share the command with him. . . . He holds all things in the world together, and preserves them in those functions wherein he settled them, and conducts them to those ends, for which he designed them. (Charnock)

A sense of the divine care and favor has been in all ages the support of the church and the consolation of godly men. No thought can enter into the mind of man, better adapted to promote its piety and peace than this—that the world is under the government of God, and all the events of our lives under the direction of his providence. (Orton)

The belief in providence is the necessary supplement to the belief in inspiration. (Westcott)

From all the acts of God as recorded in the Scriptures, we are taught that he alone is God; that he is present everywhere to sustain and govern all things; that his wisdom is infinite, his counsel settled, and his power irresistible; that he is holy, just, and good; the Lord and the Judge—but the Father and the Friend of man. (Watson's Institutes)

I adore and kiss the providence of my Lord, who knows well what is most expedient for me, and for you, and your children. (Rutherford)

A God without dominion, without providence and final causes—is nothing but fate and 'nature'. (Sir Isaac Newton)

To infer from that passage of holy Scripture, wherein God is said to have rested from his works, that there is no longer a continual production of them, would be to make a very ill use of that text. (Leibnitz)

There is an immediate and constant superintendence exercised over the whole creation, and what we term *laws of nature* are but the operations of divine power in a regular and uniform manner. (Dr. Godwin)

The philosopher, who overlooks the traces of an all-governing Deity in nature, contenting himself with the appearances of the material universe only, and the mechanical laws of motion, neglects what is most excellent; and prefers what is imperfect to what is supremely perfect, finitude to infinity; what is narrow and weak to what is unlimited and almighty; and what is perishing to what endures forever. (Maclaurin)

We cannot conceive of any reasons that can influence the Deity to exercise any providence over the world, which are not likewise reasons for extending it to all that happens in the world. (Price)

Though troubles assail,
And dangers affright,
Though friends should all fail,
And foes all unite;
Yet one thing secures us,
Whatever betide,
The Scripture assures us—
The Lord will provide! (Newton)

Yes, You are ever present, Power Supreme!
Not circumscribed by Time, nor fixed to Space,
Confined to altars, nor to temples bound,
In Wealth, in Want, in Freedom or in Chains,
In Dungeons or on Thrones, the faithful find you! (Hannah More)

We believe that all things, both in heaven and in earth, and in all creatures—are sustained and governed by the providence of this wise, eternal, and omnipotent God. (Confession of Helvetia)

We believe that this most gracious and mighty God, after he had made all things left them not to be ruled by chance or fortune—but he himself does so continually rule and govern them, according to the prescript rule of his holy will, that nothing can happen in this world without his decree or ordinance. (Confession of Belgia)

We believe, that God made all things by his everlasting Word, that is, by his only begotten Son; and that he upholds and works all things by his Spirit, that is by his own power—and therefore that God as he has created, so he foresees and governs all things. (Confession of Basle)

When men bring themselves to think that Jehovah is too great a being to interfere in the affairs of this lower world, they are prepared, by this infidel sentiment, to adopt any evil course which may suggest itself to the depraved inclinations of the human heart. (Morison)

***God reigns* is a logical conclusion from *God is*. To deny God's providence is as atheistic as to deny his existence. A God, who neither sees, nor hears, nor knows, nor cares, nor helps, nor saves—is a vanity, and can never claim homage from intelligent men. Such a God should be derided, not worshiped. He might suit the mythology of Paganism, or meet the demands of an infidel heart—but could never command the allegiance, or win the confidence of an enlightened and pious man!**

Yet there have been and still are, those who deny Providence. "They encourage each other in evil plans, they talk about hiding their snares; they say—Who will see them?" Psalm 64:5 Some say outright, "The wicked say to themselves--'God isn't watching! He will never notice!' Arise, O Lord! Punish the wicked, O God!" Psalm 10:11-12. **Nothing more derogatory to the character of God can possibly be said, than that he does not rule the world.** To bring into existence and then forsake a race of beings, and care no more for them would argue a total lack of the moral attributes of divinity. **Such conduct may well comport with the character of false gods—but is wholly abhorrent to the nature of Jehovah. The world may as well be without a God, as have one who is incompetent to rule it, or, who, wrapping himself in a mantle of careless indifference, abandons creation to the governance of puny mortals, to the rule of devils, or to the sway of a blind chance!**

"The ostrich lays her eggs on top of the earth, letting them be warmed in the dust. She doesn't worry that a foot might crush them or that wild animals might destroy them. She is harsh toward her young, as if they were not her own. She is unconcerned though they die." Job 39:14-16. Thus this bird fulfills the instincts of her nature. Yet in so doing she proves that she is one of the lowest orders of irrational animals. But **God's tender mercies are over all his works. His kingdom rules over all.**

"Hallelujah! For the Lord our God, the Almighty, reigns!" Revelation 19:6

"Our God is in heaven and does whatever He pleases!" Psalm 115:3

"For I know that the Lord is great; our Lord is greater than all gods. The Lord does whatever He pleases in heaven and on earth, in the seas and all the depths!" Psalm 135:5-6

PROVIDENCE DEFINED

Providence is the care of God over created being; divine superintendence. (Johnson)

Providence is the care and superintendence which God exercises over his creatures. (Webster)

Providence is the divine superintendence over all created beings; the care of God over his creatures. (Worcester)

The doctrine of divine Providence is that *all things are sustained, directed, and controlled by God.* (Leonard Woods)

By the law of providence, I mean God's sovereign disposal of all the concerns of men in this world—in the variety, order, and manner, which he pleases—according to the rule and infinite reason of his own goodness, wisdom, righteousness, and truth. (John Owen)

The word providence is taken from the Latin, and by its etymology means foresight, not merely in the sense of seeing before—but in the sense of taking care for the future, or rather an ordering of things and events after a pre-determined and intelligent plan. It supposes **wisdom** to devise, and **power** to execute. (Bethune)

Providence is the superintendence and care which God exercises over creation. (Buck)

Providence is the care which God takes of all things, to uphold them in being and to direct them to the ends which he has determined to accomplish by them, so that nothing takes place in which he is not concerned in a manner worthy of his infinite perfections, and which is not in unison with the counsels of his will. (Dick)

God's conserving all things means his actual operation and government in preserving and continuing the being, powers, dispositions, and motions of all things. (Clarke)

The providence of God is his almighty and everywhere present power, whereby as it were by hand, he upholds and governs heaven, earth, and all creatures; so that herbs and grass, rain and drought, fruitful and barren years, food and drink, health and sickness, riches and poverty, yes, and all things come, not by chance—but by his fatherly hand. (Heidelberg Catechism)

God's works of providence are his most holy, wise, and powerful preserving and governing all his creatures and all their actions. (Westminster Assembly)

According to preceding views and to the Scriptures, God's providence consists—

1. In his preserving all that he has made. He upholds all things by the word of his power. Heb. 1:3. "All eyes look to You, and You give them their food in due time. You open Your hand and satisfy the desire of every living thing." Psalm 145:15, 16. This dependence of creatures is universal and perpetual. Could one link in the chain thereof be broken, the least evil that would follow would be annihilation.

2. In governing all that he has made. First, he restrains the creature. By the law of gravitation he keeps solid worlds in their places. By the power of his hand he withholds free agents from both natural and moral evil. Secondly, he guides his creatures. It is his voice that rolls the stars along, and marshals all the stars of heaven, and works wonders among the inhabitants of the earth. Without him atoms and planets, angels and devils, saints and sinners can do nothing.

"Our God is in heaven and does whatever He pleases!" Psalm 115:3

"For I know that the Lord is great; our Lord is greater than all gods. The Lord does whatever He pleases in heaven and on earth, in the seas and all the depths!" Psalm 135:5-6

"Hallelujah! For the Lord our God, the Almighty, reigns!" Revelation 19:6

God's providence results from his nature. It is holy, just, benevolent, wise, supreme and sovereign, sure and stable, powerful and irresistible.

The unrenewed heart is atheistic in its inclinations. It does not like to retain God in its thoughts. The Epicurean doctrine, that God is too exalted to notice the affairs of men, naturally flows from the ignorance and enmity of the carnal mind. But "shall I not do as I please with my own?" is the challenge of the Almighty. To manage the affairs of the universe cannot disturb God's divine tranquility. To him who made all things by the word of his power, the care of them cannot be burdensome. God is not like man. He never grows weary. That he has a right to establish an all-pervading government over his creatures is as certain as that he has any rights at all. Were our hearts not wrong—we would glory in his providence; and were our minds not feeble and our faculties not limited—we would see that all objection to God's providential care of the world was worse than frivolous.

In this age it is commonly admitted that the Lord lives and rules in the kingdoms of men. This is the avowed *theory*. The *practical belief* of many is quite diverse. There are not a few whose prevailing plans and fears and hopes, would hardly be more *practically atheistic* if they should avow disbelief of God's existence and of the divine government over human affairs. Were God, in open day, before their eyes, miraculously to suspend the laws of nature, they might for a time, perhaps, be impressed and confess that here was the finger of God. It is probable, however, that this impression would not be lasting. For in his ceaseless support and maintenance of the course of nature—such men perceive nothing to admire, nothing to adore. Were the hand which moves all worlds to arrest the sun in the heavens and cause it to stand still for even an hour, they might say, This is the Lord. But the sun may rise, and run his course, and duly set three hundred and sixty-five times in the year—and nothing is said or thought of him, at whose rebuke the pillars of heaven tremble, and by whose ordinance the everlasting mountains and the order of universal nature have their stability. "A brutish man knows not, neither does a fool understand." Psalm 92:6. Such men virtually or actually say—The Lord doesn't see it. The God of Jacob doesn't pay attention." Psalm 94:7. "The wicked say to themselves--'God isn't watching! He will never notice!' Arise, O Lord! Punish the wicked, O God!" Psalm 10:11-12. To correct such errors is one object of revelation. Scripture puts the stamp of wickedness on all such thoughts as allow men to believe that they may act independently of God.

God is above all law, being himself absolutely independent and supreme. His own infinitely excellent nature is the law of his being and of his action. This very nature fits him in all respects to be the ruler of the world.

God's providence is HOLY. Because God is holy, his providence is holy in all its works. He plots no mischief, works no evil, favors no sin; but in the winding up of human affairs, he will bring a terrible overthrow on all the workers of iniquity. He hates sin with a perfect hatred. To him it is a horrible thing. Jer. 5:30. It cannot be proven that God hates anything but sin. Nor has any mortal an adequate conception of the intensity of the aversion of the divine mind to every form and species of iniquity. "Who shall not fear you, O Lord, and glorify your name? for you alone are holy." Rev. 15:4. Indeed, the bliss of the heavenly world depends upon the absolute and unqualified confidence of saints and angels in the infinite rectitude of God's nature. Isaiah 6:3. "The Lord is righteous in all his ways, and holy in all his works." Psalm 145:17.

God's providence is JUST. From God's holiness necessarily results his justice. Dr. Woods, "The plan of providence is such that sin will be stigmatized and sinners punished, while holiness will be honored, and those who are holy rewarded." Justice is certainly an amiable attribute in any person or government. By a fiction of law under the British Constitution, "The king can do no wrong." The reason is that his ministers are responsible. But it is no fiction of law or theology that the Judge of all the earth can only do right. Gen. 18:25. In the worship of the temple not made with hands, they sing, "Great and marvelous are your works, Lord God Almighty; just and true are your ways, O King of saints." Rev. 15:3.

God's providence is BENEVOLENT. Indeed, God's tender mercies are over all his works. Psalm 145:9. "The same benevolence, which prompted him to create the world, must prompt him to preserve and govern it." "When we consider the care of providence over people, as it is manifested either in the works of nature or of grace, we naturally fall into the reflection, 'What is man, that you are mindful of him? and the son of man, that you visit him?' and we wonder to see so much done for men, who seem to have no merit or desert equal to the concern showed for them."

God's providence is WISE. In it are no gaps, no failures, no mistakes, no oversights. "The same wisdom which contrived such a wonderful and glorious a system—can and will direct and control it." God's plans embrace all causes and all effects, all facts and all contingencies, all actions and all words. Therefore it is impossible that he should be thwarted. It is infinitely easy for him to take the wise in their own craftiness. Pharaoh, the greatest monarch of his time, one whose kingdom embraced much of the wealth, learning, and civilization of the world, and who was surrounded by able men—said to his council of state, "Come on, let us deal wisely with them." Ex. 1:10. They formed their plans. Yet, from first to last they were encompassed with difficulties. And they were followed by terrific judgments. Go now and stand with Moses and Aaron and Miriam on the banks of the Red Sea, and behold the end of all their 'wise plans.' Pharaoh's army and his chosen captains have perished. The depths have covered them—they sank to the bottom as a stone—they sank as lead in the mighty waters. All the amazing operations of vegetation are by inspired men ascribed to the Lord of hosts, which is wonderful in counsel and excellent in working. Isaiah 28:29. "O Lord, how manifold are your works! in wisdom have you made them all; the earth is full of your riches. So is this great and wide sea, wherein are things creeping innumerable, both small and great beasts." Psalm 104:24, 25.

God's providence is SUPREME, and therefore SOVEREIGN. It is over all and above all. He has no divided dominion. He is sole arbiter of events and destinies. He says, "See now that I, even I, am he, and there is no God with me—I kill, and I make alive; I wound, and I heal—neither is there any that can deliver out of my hand." Deut. 32:39. "I am the first, and I am the last; and besides me there is no God." Isaiah 44:6. "I am the Lord, and there is none else, there is no God beside me, . . . there is no God else beside me—a just God and a Savior; there is none beside me." Isaiah 45:5, 21. So that it is as clear that God rules alone—as that he rules at all; that he rules everywhere—as that he rules anywhere; that he governs all agents, all causes, and all events—as that he governs any of them!

To surrender in whole or in part, his control of the universe would be to admit that he was not God—that another was as strong, as wise, or as good as himself. Isaiah 41:23. It would argue some defect in him, who has all perfection. An angel would be burdened with the sole charge of one man; because an angel is a finite creature, and has none but derived attributes. But the care of the universe is no burden to the Almighty—because he is God! His will is the law of all worlds. He stretched out the earth above the waters. "For I know that the Lord is great; our Lord is greater than all gods. The Lord does whatever He pleases in heaven and on earth, in the seas and all the depths!" Psalm 135:5-6. "All the inhabitants of the earth are reputed as nothing—and he does according to his will in the army of heaven, and among the inhabitants of the earth—and none can stay his hand, or say unto him, What do you?" Dan. 4:35. "The Lord is high above all nations, and his glory above the heavens." Psalm 113:4. "Our God is in heaven and does whatever He pleases!" Psalm 115:3.

God's providence is SURE and STABLE. Whoever wishes to walk securely, needs but to conform himself to its settled provisions and principles. Proverbs 10:9. Never did his Word fail. Greatly was the Psalmist comforted with this view of the stability of God's government, "Forever, O Lord, your word is settled in heaven. Your faithfulness is unto all generations—you have established the earth, and it abides. They continue this day according to your ordinances; for all are your servants." Psalm 119:89-91; compare Proverbs 19:21 and Josh. 23:14.

God's providence is POWERFUL and IRRESISTIBLE. His providence not only consults—it also executes. It not only devises—it also puts into operation. It not only sees how evil may be prevented—it also prevents evil. It is so powerful that it even brings good out of evil—making wicked men and fallen angels to serve God's designs, while they intend no such thing. It is so powerful that it gives the greatest efficiency to causes apparently the most contemptible; and infallibly secures the accomplishment of the very best ends. The author of Providence is "the Lord, who is, and who was, and who is to come—the Almighty." Rev. 1:8.

All the other attributes of God would not avail us—if he had not omnipotence, whereby to enforce and execute his will. All other properties of his providence would fail to give effectual consolation—if it lacked divine power. No marvel therefore that the Scriptures so frequently celebrate the triumphs of Omnipotence. Otherwise the wicked would say—Where is their rock in whom they have trusted? As to the Assyrian, so to every foe, Jehovah says, "Because your raging against Me and your arrogance have reached My ears, I will put My hook in your nose and My bit in your mouth; I will make you go back the way you came." 2 Kings 19:28. It will be for an everlasting rejoicing to all the righteous that when God makes a covenant of peace with his people, he is able to cause the evil beasts to cease out of the land—so that his people may dwell safely in the wilderness, and sleep in the woods. By his almighty power he brings mariners out of their distresses. He makes the storm a calm, so that the waves are still. All conspiracies and combinations against God's providence are vain!

GOD'S PROVIDENCE IS UNIVERSAL

God's providence is over all creatures; over fixed and planetary stars; over angels and devils; over saints and sinners; over animals, and birds, and fish; over globes and atoms; over heat and cold; over war, famine and pestilence; over heaven, earth, and hell. Having enumerated the living creatures that God has made, the psalmist says, "All of them wait for You to give them their food at the right time. When You give it to them, they gather it; when You open Your hand, they are satisfied with good things. When You hide Your face, they are terrified; when You take away their breath, they die and return to the dust. When You send Your breath, they are created, and You renew the face of the earth." Psalm 104:27-30. "Every good gift and every perfect gift is from above, and comes down from the Father of lights." James 1:17. "For who makes you different from anyone else? What do you have that you did not receive?" 1 Cor. 4:7. It is because of this universal providence of God that his people cry, "Be not far from me, O Lord—O my strength, hasten to help me." Psalm 22:19. And every pious man cries, "My cup runs over," and "He loads me daily with benefits." Psalm 23:5; 68:19. Where is the man that can number up either his sins; or what are still more numerous, God's mercies to him? Compare Dan. 4:35.

God's providence is also over all the actions of all creatures. If anyone could act independently, he would be a God. If Jehovah does not govern a man for a day, that day the man is a God. Independence is one of the essential attributes of Jehovah. Whoever has it is God. To put a single act of any creature beyond divine control would be an admission that besides the Most High there is some other God. Satan could do nothing against the holy man of Uz until the Almighty granted him permission. Job 1:12.

The Bible adopts two methods of teaching the universality of God's providence. In one it asserts it as a great truth. "He is a great King over all the earth." Psalm 47:2. "His kingdom rules over all." Psalm 103:19. "By him all things are held together." Col. 1:17. "He upholds all things by the word of his power." Heb. 1:3. "He has on his vesture and on his thigh a name written, King of kings and Lord of lords." Rev. 19:16. To him death and hell have no covering. Job 26:6.

Again the Scripture descends to particulars, and declares that over each being and event, God exercises sovereign control. "Can the One who shaped the ear not hear; the One who formed the eye not see? The One who instructs nations, the One who teaches man knowledge—does He not discipline?" Psalm 94:9-10. He never slumbers, nor sleeps, nor goes on a journey. He is ever awake. His ear is ever open to the cry of his people. He is never sick, never weary. He faints not. His eyes are in every place, beholding the evil and the good. He numbers the very hairs of our heads. Not a sparrow falls to the ground without his notice. He looks to the ends of the earth, and sees under the whole heaven. "He looks to the ends of the earth and sees everything under the heavens. When God fixed the weight of the wind and limited the water by measure, when He established a limit for the rain and a path for the lightning." Job 28:24-26. He directs journeys and makes them prosperous. 1 Thes. 3:11; Romans 1:10. He causes the grass to grow for the cattle, and herb for the service of man. Psalm 104:14. He does not cattle to decrease. Psalm 107:38. He "covers the sky with clouds, prepares rain for the earth, and causes grass to grow on the hills. He provides the animals with their food, and the young ravens, what they cry for." Psalms 147:8-9

He calls the stars by their names. He marshaled all the host of heaven. He spreads the clouds in the heaven. He is the father of the rain. He clothes the grass. He gives snow like wool. He scatters the hoarfrost like ashes. Who can stand before his cold? He hunts the prey for the lion. He sends out the wild donkey free. He gives the beautiful feathers to the peacock and plumes every fowl of heaven. He gives the horse his strength, and clothes his neck with thunder. He shuts up the sea with doors that it breaks not forth. He enters into the springs of the sea. He knows the place and the bounds of light and of darkness. Angels, men, sun, moon, stars, fiery meteors, the heavens, the waters beneath us, dragons, fire, hail, snow, vapor, stormy winds, mountains, hills, trees, beasts, cattle, creeping things, flying fowl, kings, counselors, senators, all people, young men and maidens, old men and children, lightning and earthquakes—all, all obey his voice and do his will.

Nothing ever goes beyond his grasp. Under his control the race is not to the swift, nor the battle to the strong, nor bread to the wise, nor riches to the prudent, nor favor to men of skill. Promotion comes neither from the east, nor from the west, nor from the south—but God is judge of all. Whom he will, he exalts; whom he will, he abases; whom he will, he kills; whom he will, he makes alive. As a partridge sits upon eggs and hatches them not, so is man in all his cares and toils without God's blessing. Under his government a horse is a vain thing for safety, nor shall he deliver any by his great strength. He delights not in the power of a man. Without him nothing is holy, without him nothing is wise, without him nothing is strong. He is a rock.

To us many things happen by chance. We neither foresee nor design them. We neither expect nor desire them. To us much is accident. The Scriptures so admit. Deut. 22:6; 1 Sam. 6:9; 2 Sam. 1:6; Luke 10:31. Indeed, the Bible says in so many words that time and chance happen to all. Eccles. 9:11. But to God, everything is part of a universal plan. "The lot is cast into the lap—but the whole disposing thereof is of the Lord." Proverbs 16:33. When the cup of Ahab's iniquity was full, and God determined to call him to judgment, a man "drew a bow at a venture, and smote him between the joints of the armor;" and he died. God can kill without instruments, or with instruments which seem to us despicable. So also he can save by many, by few, or by none. Under the shadow of his wings the darkest conspiracies can do us no harm. The belief of this made David say, "The Lord is my light and my salvation—whom should I fear? The Lord is the stronghold of my life—of whom should I be afraid? When evildoers came against me to devour my flesh, my foes and my enemies stumbled and fell. Though an army deploy against me, my heart is not afraid; though war breaks out against me, still I am confident." Psalm 27:1-3. And when he was old he said, "You have covered my head in the day of battle." "By you have I run through a troop—by my God have I leaped over a wall." 2 Sam. 22:30. David always ascribed his victory over the bear and the lion to the wonderful providence of God; and well he should, for he was but a lad when he slew them.

Beza somewhere mentions no less than six hundred wonderful acts of providence towards himself in the troublous times, in which he lived. In that terrible battle, when by his folly and obstinacy Braddock was both defeated and mortally wounded, a savage deliberately aimed his deadly rifle seventeen times against Washington, yet not a ball hit him. Even the Indian was struck with amazement and said, "The great Spirit will not let that man be hurt." Compare 1 Chron. 18:31, and Proverbs 16:7.

Man is immortal until his work is done.

Cyrus was king of Persia and captor of Babylon. Two centuries before his birth God thus spoke concerning him, "I call you by your name, because of Jacob My servant and Israel My chosen one. I give a name to you, though you do not know Me. I am the Lord, and there is no other; there is no God but Me. I will strengthen you, though you do not know Me, so that all may know from the rising of the sun to its setting that there is no one but Me. I am the Lord, and there is no other. I form light and create darkness, I make success and create disaster; I, the Lord, do all these things" Isaiah 45:4-7.

Again says God by Amos (3:6) "If a disaster occurs in a city, hasn't the Lord done it?" Death is God's servant. The pestilence is his rod. The wicked are his sword. Famine is his scourge. If the earth becomes iron and the heavens brass, and glow like a furnace, it is at the bidding of God. If blight and mildew, the caterpillar and the palmer-worm cut off the hope of the farmer, they are the messengers of the Lord Almighty. Death and hell have no power but from him. He carries the keys of them both. He opens and none can shut. He shuts and none can open. His wisdom is unsearchable. There is none like him. His providence is felt everywhere. He rules all men good and bad, great and small. "The king's heart is in the hand of the Lord; he directs it like a watercourse wherever he pleases." Proverbs 21:1. The reference in this text is to the custom of irrigating gardens by conducting the water in little canals, which can easily be closed, so that the gardener makes the water run in any direction he pleases. In like manner God controls the heart of the king and of every man, as the gardener checks and controls these little rivers of water. Phil. 2:13.

God could not surely defend and protect his people—if their enemies were not within his grasp. It does not impair free agency for God to present an irresistible motive either to a godly man or to a wicked man. With the former the fear of God has power sufficient to restrain him from sin. With the wicked, regard to health, honor, or wealth, have restraining power. In neither case is there a suspension of free agency. If God does not sway the hearts of the wicked so as to secure their doing that which He has determined to effect or permit, are they not independent beings? But the Scripture leaves no room for doubt on this point. Acts 2:23; 4:28; 2 Sam. 17:14. If any man were independent of God, then the promise of Satan to our first parents would be fulfilled, and men would become as gods. But the Scriptures are explicit, "The king's heart is in the hand of the Lord; he directs it like a watercourse wherever he pleases." "A man's heart devises his way—but the

Lord directs his steps." "Man's goings are of the Lord, how then can a man understand his way?" Proverbs 21:1; 16:9; 20:24.

It was the Lord that "turned the heart of the Egyptians to deal harshly with his servants." Psalm 105:25. It is also said of the Jews that the Lord "caused them to be pitied by all who held them captive." Psalm 106:46. Because God controls the free acts of wicked men, it came to pass that the vacillating Pilate, who pronounced Jesus Christ innocent, was yet prevailed on to deliver him to death—but was as firm as a rock in refusing to alter the inscription on his cross, saying, "What I have written, I have written." When Shimei cursed David, that holy man said, "Let him alone, and let him curse; for the Lord has bidden him." 2 Sam. 16:11. God took away restraint from the evil heart of that vile dog, and let him loose to bark at the royal fugitive. So the pious Jeremiah devoutly said, "O Lord, I know that the way of man is not in himself; it is not in man, who walks, to direct his steps." Therefore, if men hate and vex us, it is because the Lord removes restraints and lets them loose upon us.

When God planted the Jews in Canaan, he told them that all, who were able, must go up to the holy city three times every year to worship him. They had wicked enemies all around them, who cordially hated them, and desired their extermination. But God said, "Neither shall any man desire your land, when you shall go up to appear before the Lord your God thrice in the year." Ex. 34:24. This promise was well kept in all their generations. But this could only be by Jehovah putting his almighty hand on the hearts of the nations, and softening for the time their animosities against his people. God can make even the worst of men not to wish us any harm, and yet they may all the time be perfectly conscious of free agency. God led Absalom and his coconspirators to choose foolish rather than wise counsel, whereby their wicked plot was utterly defeated. 2 Sam. 17:14. Whenever the Lord wills, "he turns wise men backward." Isaiah 44:25. He causes bad men to punish themselves. Thus sang David, "The nations have fallen into the pit they have dug; their feet are caught in the net they have hidden. The Lord is known by his justice; the wicked are ensnared by the work of their hands" Psalm 9:15, 16.

The punishment of the wicked is thus terribly portrayed, "The evil deeds of a wicked man ensnare him; the cords of his sin hold him fast. He will die for lack of discipline, led astray by his own great folly." Proverbs 5:22, 23. "They that sow to the flesh shall of the flesh reap corruption." Gal. 6:8.

So also God uses the wicked to punish each other, and then for their own wickedness he punishes them. Thus when the Jews apostatized and became sadly degenerate, decreeing unrighteousness and writing grievousness, to turn aside the needy from judgment, and to take away the right from the poor, that widows might be their prey, and that they might rob the fatherless, God sent a mighty heathen prince to punish them. This is his prophetic address to that haughty and terrible monarch, "Woe to the Assyrian, the rod of my anger, in whose hand is the club of my wrath! I send him against a godless nation, I dispatch him against a people who anger me, to seize loot and snatch plunder, and to trample them down like mud in the streets. But this is not what he intends, this is not what he has in mind; his purpose is to destroy, to put an end to many nations. When the Lord has finished all his work against Mount Zion and Jerusalem, he will say—I will punish the king of Assyria for the willful pride of his heart and the haughty look in his eyes. Does the ax raise itself above him who swings it, or the saw boast against him who uses it? As if a rod were to wield him who lifts it up, or a club brandish him who is not wood!" Isaiah 10:5, 6, 7, 12, 15.

Thus God "makes the wrath of man to praise him, and the remainder of wrath he will restrain." He permitted men and devils to combine for the death of Jesus Christ, yet out of that event he has brought eternal redemption to countless millions, and eternal glory to the Godhead. But when they combined to keep him in the tomb, it was not possible that he should be held of death. Their malice and machinations were impotent. He burst the bars of the grave, arose by his own power and ascended up on high, leading captivity captive. Nor should this doctrine offend anyone. When Pilate said to Jesus, "Know you not that I have power to crucify you, and have power to release you?" Jesus answered, "You could have no power at all against me, except it were given you from above." John 19:10, 11. Nor does this doctrine destroy a just accountability—but rather establishes it. The very next words of Jesus are, "Therefore he who delivered me unto you has the greater sin;" thus clearly declaring that though the sin might seem to him small, yet it was sin.

Indeed if God does not hold the hearts of the wicked in his hands, and entirely control them, how can the pious pray for deliverance from wicked men with any hope that they will be heard and answered? But believing this doctrine, they may well ask God to save them, knowing that if he chooses, he can make their enemies to be their friends, and their persecutors to be their deliverers. This he has often done. This he still does, sending his people's foes bowing unto them. He, who made the raven feed Elijah, can never be at a loss for instruments of good to his chosen people, or of wrath to his enemies. If it was not beneath him to make an insect or a world, it is not beneath him to govern them to wise and holy ends.

If he should resign his control over anything even for an hour, no mortal can trace the consequences. And if he were utterly to forsake any work of his hands, no creature can calculate the mischief that would ensue; for in him we live and move and have our being. So that he alone is "Lord of all." Demons, as tempters, have mighty influence; but the feeblest child of God, clad in innocence, upheld by grace, and guided by Providence—need not fear a million demons. Satan is bound with a chain. He is the proprietor of nothing. Though he is called the God of this world and the spirit that works in the children of disobedience; yet the meaning of such language is that the desires and motives and aims and hearts of the men of this world are pleasing to Satan, who is at the head of the kingdom of darkness, and who sways a scepter of malignant power over the ungodly. Blessed be God, he has not abandoned the world, bad as it is, to the reign of demons.

Nor has God resigned any part of his government to fate or chance, both of which are blind, and have no intelligence, and of course no wisdom. He governs by a plan, which is never altered—simply because it is his plan, and therefore can never be improved. Both fate and chance as agents are nothing, and know nothing, and can do nothing. Over all the earth presides one who has all and infinite perfections. Just such a supreme ruler as the pious mind would desire for all the world, just such a ruler it now has and ever shall have.

Glory be to the Father, and to the Son, and to the Holy Spirit—as it was in the beginning, is now, and shall be evermore. Amen.

PRACTICAL REMARKS ON THE NATURE OF GOD'S PROVIDENCE

Truth is in order to godliness. The truth respecting providence is of great practical utility and calls for devout and reverent use and consideration. Sound doctrine on this subject may be as wickedly perverted as on any other matter of revelation. Let all men beware that they do not hold the truth in unrighteousness. Some of the practical considerations arising from the whole subject will be more appropriately presented hereafter. A few points urge themselves upon our attention at this time.

I. Let us firmly believe that God reigns. He is the Judge of all the earth. This is a great truth. It cannot be too boldly asserted, or too firmly believed. It is at the foundation of all true religion, of all solid peace, and of all holy living. We may not deny it. We may not even doubt it. Hos. 14:9. There is an absolute necessity for God's government over the world, and for our believing that he does control it.

We begin life without wisdom, or experience. We take many of the most important steps in life when maturity has not chastened our minds into sobriety. False notions of things, and strong passions, and subtle enemies beset us on every side, especially until after the period, when the elements of character have been pretty firmly united. If God does not preserve at such times, it is clear we must fall.

And what a **comfort** it is to believe this doctrine. If we are poor, or sick, or bereaved, or defamed, how delightful it is to know that it is the Lord, and not man; the Lord and not Satan; a friend and not an enemy; a most tender father and not a capricious master—who thus ordains. David was wise when he said, "Let me fall into the hand of the Lord, and not into the hand of man." Luther said, "Smite, Lord, for you love me." Every child of God may say as much. God himself says, "As many as I love I rebuke and chasten."

This doctrine of providence is a great pillar of hope to all godly men. The three young Hebrews believed it when they said, "Nebuchadnezzar, we don't need to give you an answer to this question. If the God we serve exists, then He can rescue us from the furnace of blazing fire, and He can rescue us from the power of you, the king. But even if He does not rescue us, we want you as king to know that we will not serve your gods or worship the gold statue you set up." Dan. 3:16-18. This is the proper fruit of this doctrine. It emboldens the timid. It confirms the wavering. It converts cowards into heroes. It makes the simple wise. It represses rashness. It keeps alive a solemn sense of responsibility. It is a rock of strength. But it must be steadfastly believed.

Dr. Dick, "As the doctrine of a particular providence is agreeable both to Scripture and to reason, so it is recommended by its obvious tendency to promote the piety and the consolation of mankind . . . The thought, that he 'compasses our paths, and is acquainted with all our ways;' that he watches our steps, orders all the events in our lot, guides and protects us, and supplies our needs, as it were with his own hand; this thought awakens a train of sentiments and feelings, highly favorable to devotion, and sheds a cheering light upon the path of life. We consider him as our guardian and our Father; and reposing upon his care, we are assured that, if we trust in him, no evil shall befall us, and no real blessing shall be withheld."

Price, "Where can be the difficulty of believing an invisible hand—a universal and ever attentive Providence, which guides all things agreeably to perfect rectitude and wisdom, at the same time that the general laws of the world are left unviolated, and the liberty of moral agents is preserved?"

"The Lord will reign forever. O Jerusalem, your God is King in every generation! Praise the Lord!" Psalm 146:10.

II. Let us not be curious in prying into inscrutable secrets connected with providence. We know but little of the little which may be known. Humbly to study providence is a duty. Boldly to pry into it is a sin. He, who cannot swim, ought not to venture into deep waters. God's ruling the world is a deep matter. Many both prejudge and misjudge all that he does. Judge nothing before the time. Remember "it is the glory of God to conceal a thing." Proverbs 25:2. But "vain man would be wise, though he be born like a wild donkey's colt." Job 11:12. The thirty-eighth, thirty-ninth, fortieth, and forty-first chapters of Job contain terrible reproofs even to godly men, who had indulged in daring speculations on divine providence. Oh, for the sublime wisdom of Paul, who stood and adoringly said, "O, the depth of the riches both of the wisdom and knowledge of God! how unsearchable are his judgments, and his ways past finding out." Why will men become cavilers and subject themselves to the alarming reproof, "Nay, but, O man, who are you that replies against God? Shall the thing formed say to him that formed it—Why have you made me thus?" The ignorance of a wise man is better than the knowledge of a fool.

III. Consider how great is the danger of resisting providence. Whenever God's will is known, submit to it, not grudgingly—but of a cheerful mind. For their sins the Jews had a hard bondage in Babylon. What made their case worse was that among them were prophets and diviners, who fomented rebellion against their masters. They were quite opposed to the reigning powers, and, in fact, were in favor of sullen rebellion against God and man. These false teachers vexed the people and kept their tempers chafed. But by God's direction, good Jeremiah wrote them a letter, saying, "The Lord Almighty, the God of Israel, sends this message to all the captives he has exiled to Babylon from Jerusalem: 'Build homes, and plan to stay. Plant gardens, and eat the food you produce. Marry, and have children. Then find spouses for them, and have many grandchildren. Multiply! Do not dwindle away! And work for the peace and prosperity of Babylon. Pray to the Lord for that city where you are held captive, for if Babylon has peace, so will you.' The Lord Almighty, the God of Israel, says, 'Do not let the prophets and mediums who are there in Babylon trick you. Do not listen to their dreams because they prophesy lies in my name. I have not sent them,' says the Lord." Jeremiah 29:4-9

How much better it is thus cheerfully to submit to Providence than to quarrel with it, and fret, and lose our good tempers, and, with our tempers, our good consciences! For "who has hardened himself against God and prospered?" Job 9:4. Let the potsherd strive with the potsherds of the earth—but woe to him that strives with his Maker. Isaiah 45:9. We are not fit to choose for ourselves. We are blind and cannot see afar off. But God sees and declares the end from the beginning. He is all-wise. He knows all the possible relations of things. "The meek will he guide in judgment." "Be not as the horse and the mule, which have no understanding, whose mouth must be held in with bit and bridle." Do not barely submit—but heartily acquiesce. If it seems hard to say, 'Not my will—but your will be done, O God'—still say it and hold your conscience firmly bound to approve it. "Commit your works unto the Lord, and your thoughts shall be established." Proverbs 16:3.

Judge not the Lord by feeble sense,
But trust Him for his grace;
Behind a frowning providence,
He hides a smiling face.

His purposes will ripen fast,
Unfolding every hour;
The bud may have a bitter taste,
But sweet will be the flower.

Blind unbelief is sure to err,
And scan his work in vain;
God is his own interpreter,
And He will make it plain.

"If I can have my God to go before me in the pillar and the cloud," said Simeon to Haldane, "I long exceedingly to visit you once more; but if I cannot see my way clear, I am better where I am."

GOD'S PROVIDENCE IS RETRIBUTIVE

"Do not be deceived: God cannot be mocked. A man reaps what he sows." Galatians 6:7. Johnson defines retribution to be a return suitable to the action. Its general import is requital or recompense. Foster says, "Retribution is one of the grand principles in the divine administration of human affairs; a requital is imperceptible only to the willfully unobservant. There is everywhere the working of the everlasting law of requital—man always gets as he gives." Although God's government is perfect in principle and in conduct, yet the work of requital, because unfinished, is not perfect in time. Augustine, "If no sin were punished here, no providence would be believed; if every sin were punished here, no judgment would be expected."

Retribution results from all the principles of the divine government already considered. There is no flaw in it. There is no injustice in it. God will not clear the guilty. He will not condemn the innocent. He will not slay the righteous with the wicked. He never confounds things that are different. He will not permit the righteous to be punished as the wicked. For a season his procedure may be inexplicable—but in the end God will abase the proud and exalt the humble; rebuke the sinner and encourage the saint.

To a remarkable degree men are made to reap what they have sown, to gather what they have strewed, and to eat the fruit of their own doings. *Like for like* is an all-pervading principle of God's government. Retribution in kind is seen in all his finished dispensations.

In its operation this principle extends to both good and bad acts. They who sow to the Spirit, shall from the Spirit reap life everlasting. They who sow to the flesh, shall from the flesh reap corruption. Covetousness heaps treasure together as fire and fuel against the last day. Christian charity transports it to Paradise to be enjoyed after death.

Requital extends to the actions of both saints and sinners. God does not overlook wrong in any of his children. In their case wastefulness brings poverty, even as with the wicked. On the other hand, industry and frugality in worldly men are commonly followed by thrift and plenty, even as with the righteous. The doctrine of retribution is essentially connected with that of accountability. It is often stated in the word of God. In the law of Moses it is laid down as the rule by which magistrates shall award punishments to wrongdoers in Israel. This proves that the thing is in itself right. "Eye for eye, tooth for tooth, hand for hand, foot for foot, burning for burning, wound for wound, stripe for stripe." "Breach for breach, eye for eye, tooth for tooth—as he has caused an injury in a man, so shall it be done to him again." "Life shall go for life, eye for eye, tooth for tooth, hand for hand, foot for foot." Ex. 21:24, 25; Levit. 24:20; Deut. 19:21.

Our Lord warned against two abuses of this principle. The first was that men applied it to matters of private revenge. The other was that some cruelly insisted upon the literal application of the principle in judicature when it would have been more benevolent to waive the right to demand a punishment, which, if insisted on, the magistrate was bound to inflict. The same law of Moses ordained that a false witness should be punished by being made to suffer the ill which he sought to bring on his brother. Deut. 19:19. The same law says that God "repays those who hate him to their face." Deut. 7:10. This very phrase probably implies the great principle here contended for. It is repeated, "The Lord will not be slack to him who hates him, he will repay him to his face." Deut. 7:10.

Retribution in kind is often categorically taught in Scripture. "With the faithful You prove Yourself faithful; with the blameless man You prove Yourself blameless; with the pure You prove Yourself pure, but with the crooked You prove Yourself shrewd." 2 Sam. 22:26, 27. In Psalm 18:25, 26, we have almost the same words repeated. In both cases God teaches, says Clarke, that "he will deal with men as they deal with each other. . . . The merciful, the upright, the pure will ever have the God of mercy, uprightness and purity to defend them. And he will follow the wicked through all his windings, trace him through all his crooked ways, untwist him in all his cunning wiles, and defeat all his schemes of stubbornness, fraud and deceit. . . . If you perversely oppose your Maker, he will oppose you. No work or project shall prosper, which is not begun in his name and conducted in his fear." Poole, "Man's perverseness is moral and sinful—but God's shrewdness is judicial and penal."

At the dedication of the temple Solomon prayed that in coming generations the Lord would "condemn the wicked to bring his way upon his head, and justify the righteous to give him according to his righteousness." 1 Kings 8:22. So that this very principle is inwoven with the devotions of the true Israel.

In the sermon on the mount, our Lord twice asserts the same doctrine, "Blessed are the merciful—for they shall obtain mercy;" and "For in the same way you judge others, you will be judged, and with the measure you use, it will be measured to you." Matt. 5:7; 7:2. So in Psalm 7:15, 16, of the wicked it is said, "He who digs a hole and scoops it out falls into the pit he has made. The trouble he causes recoils on himself; his violence comes down on his own head." Compare Psalm 109:17. No less clearly does Solomon assert the same thing, "Surely the Lord scorns the scorners," Proverbs 3:34; and one of the Apostles says, "He shall have judgment without mercy that has showed no mercy." James 2:13.

The same law of requital prevails respecting the good deeds of men. "Blessed is he who has regard for the weak; the Lord delivers him in times of trouble. The Lord will protect him and preserve his life; he will bless him in the land and not surrender him to the desire of his foes. The Lord will sustain him on his sickbed and restore him from his bed of illness." Psalm 41:1-3.

Thus frequently does the Scripture assert this principle in express terms. It also gives us many examples. Jehovah has often "written the cause of the judgment in the forehead of the judgment itself." The builders of Babel form a league, binding themselves together forever. The Lord dissolves the league by confounding their language, and making them a torment to each other. The Egyptians destroy the infants of the Israelites by drowning them in the Nile. In God's anger the waters of their great river are turned into blood, and finally their king and his army are drowned in the Red Sea. They delighted in drowning, so God let them have their fill of it. They delighted in overtasking the Hebrews, and exposing them to the intense heat of the brickyards. So the dust from the furnaces, where the bricks had been burned, being scattered in the air, the Egyptians were covered with boils and with blisters. Thus they were made to smart as they had made others to smart.

By fraud and deception Jacob supplants his brother. Time rolls on. Jacob leaves his native land. Far from home he often finds his wages changed. Worse than all, in the matter of marriage he is miserably deceived. He loves Rachel and cheerfully serves seven years for her; and in the hour of his rejoicing finds that Leah has been palmed off on him. Thus he is made to feel in the tenderest possible manner the nature of his own wickedness to his brother.

"If men deal treacherously with others, by and by others will deal treacherously with them."

When the Israelites took Bezek, its cruel prince, "Adoni-Bezek fled, but they chased him and caught him, and cut off his thumbs and big toes." Then this guilty man began to reason on the moral government that is executed in this world, "Seventy kings with their thumbs and big toes cut off have picked up scraps under my table. Now God has paid me back for what I did to them." Judges 1:5, 6.

The ninth chapter of Judges contains fifty-seven verses, and gives the history of the crimes and end of Abimelech, the son of Jerubbaal, who conspired with the men of Shechem for the destruction of all the children of his father, being seventy people, one only, Jotham, escaping. The awful deed was done. The rivals for power were put out of the way. For a season things seemed to prosper. Still there were difficulties. By the Spirit of God Jotham had uttered a fearful prediction respecting his bloody brother and his accomplices. Before long Abimelech himself in a cruel manner destroyed the men of Shechem. Not long after "a woman on the roof threw down a millstone that landed on Abimelech's head and crushed his skull." The conclusion of the inspired record is solemn, "Thus, God punished Abimelech for the evil he had done against his father by murdering his seventy brothers. God also punished the men of Shechem for all their evil. So the curse of Jotham son of Gideon came true." Judges 9:56-57. Fuller, "If our backslidings have consisted in unfaithfulness towards one another, God will oftentimes punish this sin by so ordering it that others shall be unfaithful to us in return."

Dreadful was the course of divine judgment towards Agag, the king of the Amalekites. By God's direction Samuel said to him, "As your sword has made women childless, so shall your mother be made childless among women. And Samuel hewed Agag in pieces before the Lord in Gilgal." 1 Sam. 15:33.

In like manner for lying to Naaman the leper of Assyria, and for lying to his master, the leprosy of Naaman cleaved unto Gehazi and unto his seed forever, and he went out from the presence of Elisha, as a leper. 2 Kings 5:20-27. Dreadful was the sin, and dreadful the punishment. Shame and misery follow a man and all his posterity through all their generations for this willful, deliberate falsehood.

History tells of horrible sufferings coming on those who delighted in inflicting horrible sufferings on others. **Nero**, who loved to shed blood, the blood of his best subjects, and especially of Christians—was condemned to be punished according to the custom of the ancient Romans. He turned executioner of their sentence, slew himself; and left the world exclaiming, "I have lived shamefully, I die more shamefully." **Domitian** first trained himself and then his minions to acts of tormenting cruelty. He was in the end murdered by his own servants. Dogs licked up the blood of **Ahab**, where he had caused them to lick up the blood of the conscientious Naboth. The same cruel prince had trained a set of men addicted to bloody deeds. So soon as he was gone, these very men rid the land of his posterity. In Cilicia A. D. 117 died **Trajan**, the persecutor. His joints were loosed. His life was drowned out by the waters of dropsy, while thirst was burning him up. His successor, **Adrian**, departed this life A. D. 139 by a disease, which took most of the blood from his body. He, who had shed innocent blood, now reluctantly and in agony shed his own blood. **Maximin** and his little son were both put to death by the servants and soldiers, whom he had educated to deeds of carnage. As they slew his child, they said, "Not a whelp of so cursed a stock shall be left." **Diocletian** became a madman. His palace was consumed by fire from heaven. His end was fearful.

Lucian derided the Christians by barking at them like a dog. His death was in this way. He was torn to pieces by the dogs. A modern tyrant and murderer prepared two cups of wine, one for himself and one for his guest. He gave special direction to his servant as to the disposition of the cups. Yet in carelessness his servant gave him the cup of poison. He drank it all, and expired in convulsions.

Charles IX of France caused the shedding of the blood of the Huguenots on St. Bartholomew's day. Voltaire tells us that the blood of that cruel prince burst through the pores of his skin. His nature was at war with itself. Several writers tell us of the old man, whose son dragged him by his gray locks to the threshold of his door, when looking up he said, "Stop, my son; this is as far as I dragged my father by his hair." For a while cruel and bloody men may seem to have it all their own way; but before long God's hand will lay hold on vengeance. They may mock and afflict the innocent. But among such, who ever lived and died happily? Sooner or later a pitiless storm beats them down.

This arrangement of Providence enables us to see and feel the justice of many things in the orderings of the Lord. Were our sufferings something foreign from our own conduct, we might often be perplexed with occurrences that happen to us. But when sorrow comes to us in the Spirit of the wrong we have committed, we say, Righteous are you, Lord God Almighty.

In the same way we learn to study the book of Providence. Its lessons are made easy and forcible. Thus also we see how just is God in his dealings. He who gets what he gives, cannot complain of wrong. It is right the murderer should feel in his own person, the pangs of the death he has inflicted on another.

In like manner God teaches us that it is an evil and a bitter thing to sin against the Lord. **There is no evil so great as sin.** By this arrangement of his providence, he makes us feel that sin is horrible.

So also we learn the folly of sin. **O what shame and confusion, running perhaps through life, come on us for one wicked deed.** Before long no doubt every sin will appear as foolish as the most silly conduct is sometimes made now to appear.

Let every man honestly and earnestly inquire in the day of adversity, Why, O Lord, do you contend with me? It is a rational and proper inquiry. He, who will not make it, must expect to be hardened under judgments.

In applying this principle of God's government to ourselves, we may be strict and even severe. Our self-love will hold us back from excess. If we are innocent, conscience will shield us. Few men are harsh in their judgments of themselves. It is far otherwise in judging of our fellow-men. We must give them the benefit of any doubt in their case. In passing the conduct of others under review we must be lenient. A charitable judgment of godly men is more apt to be true than one that is harsh.

Whenever our sin is brought to view, let us repent of it, abhor it, ask forgiveness for it and forsake it. Newton says, "If a man will make his nest below, God will put a thorn in it; and if that will not do, he will set it on fire." Beware, O man, how you behave towards God in the day of chastisement for your sins. "Get up, go away! For this is not your resting place, because it is defiled, it is ruined, beyond all remedy." Micah 2:10

Let every man be warned and deterred from courses of conduct, which by this great law of requital must yet involve him in trouble, perhaps even down to old age. Some sixty years ago there lived on the borders of civilization a man who had an aged, infirm, and blind father. The old man frequently broke the plate on which his food was served. His son's wife complained of it, and the son at last determined to take a block of wood and hew out a tray on which to feed his father. Accordingly he took his axe and went to the forest, followed by his little son. He found a poplar, that looked as if it would suit his purpose, and began to cut out a block of the desired size. Having swung his axe a few moments, he became weary, and his son said, "Father, what are you going to make?" The father replied, "I am going to make a tray for your grandfather, to eat out of." The little boy loved his grandfather very much, and supposed it all very kind, and said, "I am so glad; won't it be nice? Father, when you get to be old and blind, I will make a tray for you." The father, conscience-stricken, and fearing sorrow for himself, took up his axe, returned home, and ever after seemed to treat his aged parent kindly.

God's people are safe though his enemies are not. "For the moth shall eat them up like a garment, and the worm shall eat them like wool—but my righteousness," says God, "shall be forever, and my salvation from generation to generation." Isaiah 51:8. Temptations may assail them; enemies may revile them, and persecute them. But God says, "Hear me, you who know what is right, you people who have my law in your hearts: Do not fear the reproach of men or be terrified by their insults." Isaiah 51:7.

Let us, however, beware of the error into which Job's friends fell. "They maintained that God governed the world upon the principle of minute retribution, rendering to every man in the present life according to his works;" and that this requital was perfect in this world. Against this theory Job argued irrefragably, and God himself condemned them and approved Job, saying unto Eliphaz, "My wrath is kindled against you, and against your two friends—for you have not spoken of me the thing that is right, as my servant Job has." Job 42:7.

SOME EXPLANATION OF THE DELAYS OF PROVIDENCE IN PUNISHING THE WICKED.

HOW DIVINE PATIENCE SHOULD BE REGARDED; AND HOW IT MAY BE ABUSED.

The Almighty does not settle his accounts with creatures every thirty days. He is long-suffering. He is patient under affronts. He forbears to execute deserved wrath upon offenders. This is one of the striking displays of the goodness of God designed to lead us to repentance. He bears long with us. He is slow to anger. He is *the God of patience*. Long-suffering is of his very essence. Man may exist without being kind, and gentle, and forbearing. God cannot. He can no more cease to be pitiful than he can cease to be. He warns; he entreats; he follows with mercy the very men, who flee from his gracious presence and kind offers. Often for a long time he delays his judgments.

It is very important that we should not misunderstand God's dealings in this matter. Let us not misinterpret providence, nor fall into the errors of the wicked. A few remarks made in order may help to set the matter in a clear light.

I. let us notice some things which do not cause God to delay deserved punishment.

1. God does not defer the punishment of any sinner, because it would be unrighteous instantly to cut him down, and bring him to judgment. The sentence, "The soul that sins, it shall die"—is as just as it is alarming. Every sin deserves God's wrath and curse now and hereafter. It deserves punishment the moment it is committed. What evil there is in iniquity, is in it at the instant of perpetration. A murder does not become less or more a murder by the lapse of time. Whatever guilt there is in any sin, is in it from the first. A repetition of an offence is an additional sin. But it would be just and right in God to punish deservedly and terribly, as soon as he is insulted and offended. He did so in the case of the rebel angels.

2. Nor does God withhold his wrath, because we have not *often* offended him. Of each of us it is true that our sins are more than the hairs of our heads. They are innumerable. We cannot answer for one of a thousand of them. And each one of them calls for vengeance.

3. Nor does God exercise forbearance, because he has not at all times a distinct view of the number and aggravation of our offences. In no sense does God ever forget any sin. He always sees it, knows it, hates it. His soul abhors it. He is angry with the wicked every day. No being is so far removed from everything like insensibility to sin, as God is.

4. Nor does God delay the punishment of the wicked because they escape his notice, or elude his search; nor because he cannot prove them guilty, nor because he is not as competent to decide upon their case as he ever will be. Human governments sometimes cannot detect, arrest, or convict. Evidence may be lacking. Witnesses may be absent. The law in the case may be doubtful. But these things never cause a moment's delay in the *divine* government.

5. Nor are sinners allowed to go unpunished for a season, because God regards with indifference the false impressions, which some receive from his long-suffering. On the contrary, he "is a jealous God." He is most jealous of his honor, and carefully guards the glory of his government. He would forever part with all the creatures he has made, rather than allow one truthful charge to be brought against his justice. When the rebellion broke out in heaven—in a moment he emptied the shining seats above, rather than let one sinning angel remain in his estate, a standing reproach to God, a monument of God's tolerance of sin.

6. Nor does God refrain to punish the wicked for a time, because he has not full power to execute any sentence, which his justice might decree. Omnipotence can do anything—at any time! Human governments are sometimes afraid to punish, lest they should arouse popular indignation, or dangerous commotions. But God is not for one moment restrained from executing the fierceness of his anger by any such fear. Were the world in arms against him, He who sits in the heavens would laugh at their impotent rage. One breath, one word from Jehovah would sweep them down to hell in a moment!

7. Nor is there in the divine mind any weakness, any irresolution, any lack of determination to award to every man according as his case shall demand. Many offences among men go entirely unpunished because of the vacillation of mind or feebleness of spirit in parents, masters or rulers. But it is far otherwise with God. He proceeds to the work of judgment and of punishment with an inflexible purpose, whenever his holiness and wisdom determine that the right time has come.

Let us then

II. Consider positively—why God bears long with men. Perhaps the discussion of this point is no more important than that of the preceding. But surely there are some things involved in it, which ought to make it to us lost sinners a welcome and a delightful theme.

1. God delays to punish sinners, because in his nature are found infinite love and mercy. This thought is full of weight and of interest. Let us dwell upon it. God is "long-suffering to us," because he has a loving, pitying, compassionate nature.

A modern writer [William Nevins] has collected and compared many of the forms of expression used on this subject. He says, "There is something very special in the manner in which this doctrine is taught. Observe, *first*, several words, nearly synonymous, are used to teach us the doctrine, such as *merciful, gracious, long-suffering, pitiful, slow to anger.* And not satisfied with the positive the inspired writers use the superlative—*very pitiful* and *very gracious* also.

Observe, *secondly*, that not content with the singular, *mercy*, they adopt and employ the plural form, *mercies.* They speak of the *mercie***s** of God; nor are they content with a *simple* plural; but they speak of these mercies as *manifold*, yes, they speak of the *multitude of his mercies.* This is strange language. It expresses a conception not of human origin. And to denote that there is nothing uncertain about these mercies, they speak of them as *sure* mercies; and they speak of them not only as many but *great!* yes, and *great above* the *heavens!* And they speak of the greatness of his mercies, in *magnitude* equal to what they are in *multitude*—many and great and sure mercies. Think of that! But they are not *mere* mercies—but *tender* mercies, and these mercies they speak of not as *derived*—but as *original* with God. They speak of him as *the Father of* mercies; and they take care to tell us that mercy is not *accidental* to God—but essential; they speak of it as *belonging* to him. Daniel goes further still; he says—'To the Lord our God belong mercies' and forgiveness? No; but 'forgivenesses.' You may say that is not proper grammar—but it is glorious doctrine!

Thirdly, there is another set of phrases they use; they speak of

God as *rich* in mercy, *plenteous* in mercy, and *full of* compassion. They speak of his *abundant* mercy, of the earth as *full of his mercy*, to denote its amplitude. And in respect of its continuance, they say *his compassions fail not*, and in Psalm 136, twenty-six times it is said, *His mercy endures forever.*

There is still another phraseology used by the sacred writers. They speak of God's *kindness*, his *great* kindness, his *marvelous* kindness, his *everlasting* kindness. But they are not satisfied to speak of it as simple kindness; they call it *merciful* kindness, and speak of it as *great* towards us. They call it *loving-kindness*, also, and we read of God's *marvelous* and *excellent* loving-kindness, with which it is said also that he *crowns* us! Here, too, they use the plural form, *loving-kindnesses;* and they speak of *the multitude of his loving-kindnesses.* **What more could they say?**

Fourthly, we find the mercy of God compared to certain human exercises; for example, to a father's pity, which it is said to be like, and to a brother's friendship, than which it is closer, and to a mother's love, which it is said to exceed."

Truly, it is astonishing that such sinners as we are should be spared; but surely it is not astonishing that if spared at all, it should be under the government of *such* a God. "The Lord is long-suffering, not willing that any should perish." God never punishes with delight. He does not will, or plan, or seek the ruin of his bitterest and most inveterate enemies. In the esteem of God the death of a sinner is a dreadful thing. "Many a time he turns his anger away" (Psalm 78:38) before he strikes a blow or crushes a sinful worm. The reason is, "God is love." None else would bear so long—would so long avert deserved and terrible punishments from the heads of the rebellious. Truly, the prophet told us of the glorious nature of God, when he said, "The Lord does not afflict willingly, nor grieve the children of men."

So far as we know, there is but one thing upon which the pure and benevolent mind of God looks with more aversion than upon the misery of his creatures. That one thing is worse than all misery, more horrible than the torments of hell. It is SIN, the parent of all misery, all disorder, all confusion. Every sigh from hell and every groan from earth is wrought out by sin, man's most cruel tyrant, God's greatest enemy. Benevolent, indeed, must be the nature of Jehovah to show pity and long-suffering to sinners.

2. God delays deserved punishment, because if he did not, the race of man would immediately be extinct, and horrible desolation would seize upon all the habitable parts of the earth. In the days of Noah the long-suffering of God, after waiting a hundred and twenty years, was exhausted, and but eight souls escaped the dreadful overthrow. God has great ends to answer by the creation of the world. To sweep away all its inhabitants would defeat those glorious purposes.

3. One great purpose of God is to continue and enlarge the church of Christ upon earth. The flock of God has ever been composed of those, who, in God's esteem and in their own esteem, had once been great sinners, and so deserved dreadful judgments. Had not God patiently borne with their evil manners, there is not one member of the visible church, who would not long since have perished. So says the conscience of every renewed man.

"But I will not destroy them all," says the Lord. "For just as good grapes are found among a cluster of bad ones (and someone will say, 'Don't throw them all away—there are some good grapes there!'), so I will not destroy all Israel. For I still have true servants there." Isaiah 65:8.

4. For the sake of his people, and in answer to their prayers, many a wicked man is spared for a long time. So Jesus taught, "Except those days be shortened, there should no flesh be saved—but for the elect's sake those days shall be shortened." Ten righteous men would have saved the cities of the plain from the vengeance of eternal fire. Many a time God permits the wicked to outlive their godly parents and friends, that the pious may escape the anguish of weeping over them, when they die in their sins, in their unbelief, and in their impenitency.

5. God long spares sinners, that by his goodness they may be led to repentance. He is "not willing that any should perish—but that all should come to repentance." In subduing the hearts of sinners, God's great argument is his kindness. If God instantly punished every man according to his transgressions, we could no more be exhorted to "count the long-suffering of God salvation." Thus God teaches. So also is his practice. A right view of the divine forbearance and mercy breaks every heart that ever is broken, bows every will that ever submits. "They shall look on him whom they have pierced—and mourn."

6. God long spares sinful men that he may entirely cut off all pleas from his incorrigible foes, and make his justice glorious, when he shall at last visit them for their sins. Every murmur against God, and every suspicion of the divine equity must be banished forever, if it shall at last appear that "God endured with much long-suffering the vessels of wrath fitted to destruction," and that not until it was evident that longer forbearance would give plausibility to the charge of weakness or irresolution, did God "show his wrath and make his power known." The truth must be kept alive that "there is a God that judges in the earth." But in impressing even this truth on men Jehovah adopts a course of great long-suffering. Let us notice—

III. The proper USES of this doctrine.

1. If God is so long-suffering to us, we ought to be long-suffering to one another. No man has ever treated any of us as badly as each of us has treated God. If God spares us, let us spare one another. "Beloved, if God so loved us—we ought also to love one another." "Be kind to each other, tenderhearted, forgiving one another, just as God through Christ has forgiven you." The true spirit of the Gospel never calls down fire from heaven even on the bitterest foes. He, to whom ten thousand talents have been forgiven, is surely not the man to take his brother by the throat, and say—Pay me the fifty pence you owe!

2. When we see God sparing the lives of our wicked friends and neighbors, we ought to labor and pray for their salvation. Not only should we desire it. We should also expect it. Perhaps the church often abandons sinners before God's Spirit forsakes them. Pray and toil for their conversion while there is breath—for while there is life, there is hope. Look at the miracles of grace around you, yes, look at yourself, and be encouraged to hope and pray for others!

3. Let a due consideration of God's long-suffering increase our abhorrence of sin. All sin is an offence against the most gentle, loving, patient, forbearing Being in the universe. To maltreat any *man* is wrong. But to pursue with causeless insults, and abuse a person who shows a loving disposition, even after he has been treated amiss, is justly regarded as very despicable. Such is the real character of all the sin we commit against God. And sin in the regenerate is against more love, more light and more mercy than are granted to the unregenerate. O Christian, hate sin in all—but most of all, hate it in yourself.

4. Let the long-suffering of God lead you carefully to study, admire and imitate the character of God. Be like him. Think upon his name. Acquaint yourself with God and be at peace. His nature is love. Hell for depth, heaven for height, the ocean for vastness, the sun for brilliancy are all wonderful objects. But **God's character is a combination of all that is vast, sublime, majestic, kind, just, excellent and every way glorious.** O study the character of God.

5. Learn to be patient and even thankful amidst trials and afflictions. It does not befit us to make so much of a light affliction—when we deserve a heavy curse! Think of the kindness still shown you. "Were there but a single mercy apportioned to each moment of our lives, the sum would rise very high; but how is our arithmetic confounded when every minute has more than we can distinctly number." "Be patient, therefore, brethren, until the coming of our Lord Jesus Christ." Your sorrows may be great—but the promises and the grace secured by covenant are far greater. Therefore, "strengthen the hands which hang down, and the feeble knees." Any sinner, on whom the sentence of fiery condemnation has not been executed, has great cause of joy and gratitude to God for sparing mercy. Surely he, whose hope is set in God, ought never to be much cast down—but ought to remember that he shall yet sing the song of Moses and Miriam, yes of Moses and the Lamb!

IV. Several ways in which the long-suffering of God is perverted and abused.

1. Some, finding the wicked spared so long, infer that there is no God at all. They become atheists. There have been such monsters on earth. Reasoning more false than that—which from God's goodness infers his non-existence—can hardly be imagined!

2. A kindred error is that, when from God's patience, men infer that he is not just, and holy, and determined to deal with the wicked according to their sins. This is the great pillar, on which rest many false notions or systems of belief. He, who from God's long-suffering argues that he will clear the guilty and justify the wicked, perverts the most precious things. To the rebellious God never says, "It shall be well with you." But he does say, "Will you steal, and murder, and commit adultery, and swear falsely, and burn incense unto Baal, and walk after other gods, which you know not; and come and stand before me in this house, which is called by my name, and say, We are delivered to do all these abominations?" That is, they inferred that their conduct was not displeasing to God, because awful judgments had not swept them away. Elsewhere God says, "Because I kept silence," *that is* did not instantly and terribly reprove your wickedness, "because I kept silence you thought I was altogether such a one as yourself." Thus men deny God's attributes. "The wicked live, become old, yes, are mighty in power," not because there is not a just God—but because that just God is patient and merciful.

3. Some abuse the long-suffering of God, not only to con-

tinuing in sin—but to making themselves more vile than ever. Often did the Lord lift the curse from off the head of Pharaoh, and as often did he sin the more. He was very gracious when the pangs were upon him—but as soon as the suffering was over, his relentings were over also. "Because sentence against an evil work is not executed speedily, therefore the heart of the sons of men is fully set in them to do evil." What sad perverseness is here! The sinner says, Because God is good I will be bad; because he is slow to anger, I will walk in the evil of my own ways, and pursue the wicked desires of my heart. These thoughts may not be framed into words—but are they not carried out in the lives of many? Does not the increasing wickedness of men of uncircumcised hearts declare this as plainly as God's word itself? To all such, the following solemn thoughts are presented.

a. A final perdition wrought out under circumstances of such amazing mercy as surround you, will be far more intolerable than if your life had been shorter and your blessings fewer.

That divine clemency, which you now abuse and pervert, may, for anything you know, be nearly exhausted! When it shall be all gone, and your lamp put out in obscure darkness, how can you bear reflection on the course of life you are now pursuing?

c. If any shall be so wicked as to persist in sin and finally perish, the imputation of folly and madness will fall upon their own head. "You have destroyed yourself!" "You have procured this unto yourself!" What dreadful sentences are these!

d. The Scripture calls on all the wicked to turn and live. Will you *repent?* Will you *now* repent? That you will repent is as certain as that there is a holy and just God. But whether your repentance shall be that sorrow, which works death; or that godly sorrow which works repentance not to be repented of—is the great question. Shall your repentance be unto life and salvation? or shall it be but the fruitless relenting of a soul in an undone eternity? O accept the mercy offered to you now. Embrace the Savior, while he waits to be gracious.

SEVERAL PRINCIPLES OF THE DOCTRINE OF PROVIDENCE OVER UNGODLY MEN

ILLUSTRATED IN THE LIFE AND END OF JUDAS ISCARIOT

"While they were eating, He said, 'I assure you: One of you will betray Me.'" Matthew 26:21

"For Jesus knew from the beginning those who would not believe, and the one who would betray Him." John 6:64

"For He knew who would betray Him." John 13:11

Christ's ministers are often deceived; Christ, never. He knows all things. He is never outsmarted. His eyes are as flaming fire. He easily detects the most sophisticated pretenses. He knows all men, all hearts, all destinies.

In many ways he proved all this when on earth. In the case of the *son of perdition* he fully showed that he was not for a moment mistaken in his character. It is proposed to show how the course of providence ran towards this wicked man. In order to effect that object, it is best to begin with—

I. The history of Judas.

His name was Judas, and his surname was Iscariot. Judas, Juda, Judah, Jehudah, and Jude are all the same word, varied only in unimportant particulars. The word Judas literally signifies, the praise of the Lord. The name was common among the Israelites. One of Jacob's sons was called Judah. From him descended the tribe, within whose territory was Jerusalem, and from which arose the name of Jews. After the ten tribes broke off, Judah designated the tribes of Judah and Benjamin, while the rest were called Israel. One of the Maccabees, very renowned in history, was called Judas. Another of them, who bore the same name, suffered martyrdom under Antiochus Epiphanes. Besides these, there are several other people of the same name, more or less noticed in Jewish history before the coming of Christ. After that we have an account of four men called Judas. One was Paul's host at Damascus. Acts 9:11. Another was surnamed Barsabas. He was sent with Paul and Barnabas and Silas to carry to Antioch the decrees of the Council of Jerusalem. This was itself a high honor. Luke calls him one of the "chief men among the brethren." Acts 15:22. Another was surnamed Thaddeus, or Lebbeus, or Zelotes. In Matthew 13:55, he is called the brother (or kinsman) of our Lord. He is thought to have been the son of Mary, the sister of the blessed virgin, and the brother of James the Less. If so, he was, according to the flesh, cousin to Jesus. His father's name was Alpheus. The last epistle in the Bible bears the name of Jude, and was written by this man.

The other Judas, mentioned as living in the first century of the Christian era, is the betrayer of our Lord, surnamed Iscariot. The word Iscariot is variously derived. Some say it is an abbreviation of Issachariothes, and simply declares that he was of the tribe of Issachar. Others derive it from two Hebrew words that unitedly signify, a man of murder. Others suppose that his surname simply shows that he was of the place called Carioth or Kerioth. This is probably the true explanation. Ish-Carioth or Iscariot is literally, a man of Carioth.

Before entering into the particulars of his history, observe

1. There is no evidence that Judas Iscariot was a man of bad countenance. Most men are much influenced by looks, and many think they can tell a man's character by the physiognomy. This may often be true; but there are many exceptions. The case of Judas was probably one. In paintings intended to represent him, he is commonly distinguished by a sly, base, cunning, malicious countenance. There is nothing in Scripture to warrant artists in so painting him, beyond the simple fact of his wickedness. For anything that appears to the contrary, he was a man of calm, free, open, placid, benignant countenance.

2. There is no evidence that, up to his betrayal of his Lord, his conduct was the subject of censure, complaint, jealousy—or of the slightest suspicion. Until the night when he committed the traitorous deed, his reputation seems to have been fair, and without the shadow of a blemish. He was not ambitious, as James and John on one occasion were. He was free from the characteristic rashness of Peter. His sins were all concealed from the eyes of mortals. He was a thief; but that was known only to Omniscience.

3. There is no evidence that, during his continuance with Christ, he regarded himself as a hypocrite. Doubtless he thought himself honest. He knew no other kind of sincerity than that which he possessed. He may have had solemn and joyful feelings under

the preaching of Christ. He may have had very awful and tender thoughts when he himself was preaching. Such is man's self-ignorance, that it is probable not one in ten thousand who are hypocrites firmly believe that such is their character. Nay, it commonly happens, that **the worse men are, the better they think themselves to be.**

4. Let it not be supposed that Judas ought not to have known his character. He shut his eyes to the truth respecting himself. He voluntarily rejected evidence that would have convicted him at the bar of his own conscience. **Self-ignorance is a great sin.** It is fostered by pride and unbelief and impenitence. The first mention made of this man is entirely creditable to him. He is introduced to us as one of the twelve, whom Christ chose as disciples and confidential friends, to be with him and hear his instructions, both public and private. We are not told that Christ ever availed himself, in the absence of Judas, to make any communications to the eleven, until the night of his betrayal. Peter, James and John were more with Christ than the others. But between Judas and the other eight there does not appear to have been any marked difference in the treatment which they received at the hands of the Savior.

Having for some time been a disciple, the Lord ordained him with the other eleven to the office and work of an apostle. Matt. 10:2-4; Mark 3:13-19; Luke 6:13-16. Since the birth of Christ this is the highest office to which any mortal could attain. The gifts requisite for the performance of its duties were extraordinary and miraculous. They belong to no man now living. The proofs of an apostle were in signs, and wonders, and miracles. 2 Cor. 12:12. Every apostle must have seen the Lord. 1 Cor. 9:1. There were in early times, as there are still, vain pretenders to this office; but it is the duty and honor of the churches to expose their idle claims. Rev. 2:2. But Judas was an apostle, and performed the duties of his office as did his fellows. He preached, he healed the sick, he cleansed the lepers, he raised the dead, he cast out devils. One part of the apostolic commission required the shaking off of the dust from the feet as a testimony against those who would not receive them nor hear their words. It may be that Judas did this very thing—but there is no evidence that he was more denunciatory than others.

After the return of the apostles from their first mission, and after they had given an account of their success, there is nothing said of Judas, until James and John, at the instigation and through the instrumentality of their mother, applied for the superiority over their brethren. On this occasion, it is said, "The ten were moved with indignation against the two brethren." Matt. 20:24. Mark says, "When the ten heard it, they began to be much displeased with James and John." 10:41. The record shows no difference between the behavior of Judas and that of the nine others. They all may have spoken of the wickedness of such ambition, and their remarks may have been very just. Judas may have been as temperate as the rest. There is no evidence that he possessed a bitter or intolerant spirit beyond others, nor that he was often guilty of censoriousness. It is not at all improbable that Peter was more liable to reproof in this matter than Judas.

Soon after this, we find Christ warning his disciples against "the leaven of the Pharisees, which is hypocrisy." Luke 12:1. Judas may have improved this hint so far as to attack these arch deceivers, and to preach some very searching, alarming sermons. But as a matter of personal application to his own heart and conscience, the warning seems to have been wholly neglected. Like many modern hypocrites, he probably gloried in his sincerity. Even bold transgressors, who break all God's laws, often boast of their truth, candor and honesty.

Not very long after this, Christ made a more pointed declaration, which must have excited considerable attention. It was this, "Have I not chosen you twelve, and one of you is a devil?" John 6:70. We are not left to conjecture who was intended, for the Evangelist adds, "He spoke of Judas Iscariot, the son of Simon—for he it was who would betray him, being one of the twelve." John 6:71. Sometime after Jesus said, "You are clean—but not all. For he knew who should betray him—therefore said he, You are not all clean." John 13:10, 11. What effect these sayings may have had, we are not informed. But they do not seem to have provoked any uncharitable remarks. Even Judas seems to have remembered that Christ had said, "Judge not, that you be not judged." Matt. 7:1. But we do not learn that these warnings of Christ caused Judas to search his own heart. It is certain that they had no permanent, beneficial effect; though it is almost inconceivable that they should have been wholly powerless.

The next account we have of Judas respects his apparent regard for the poor. When the affectionate Mary anointed the feet of the blessed Jesus, Judas was there. Being treasurer of Christ's family, and acting without auditors, he had dishonestly used some of the funds for his own private purposes. Hence he is called "a thief." It is nowhere hinted, however, that he esteemed himself a rogue. He may have thought that he ought to have more than any other, as he had all the care of the finances. He may also have deceived himself with idle plans of future restitution. There is no evidence that he fully condemned himself for a moment, though he may have had qualms and misgivings. When Mary anointed the Lord, Judas objected to such an expenditure, and on grounds quite plausible to some minds, "Why was not this ointment sold for three hundred pence, and given to the poor?" John 12:5. This reasoning seems to have struck others, who were godly men. Matthew says—"The disciples had indignation, saying, To what purpose is this waste?" And Mark says—Some of those at the table were indignant. "Why was this expensive perfume wasted?" they asked. "She could have sold it for a small fortune and given the money to the poor!" And they scolded her harshly." Mark 14:4, 5. How often are godly men led astray by the specious pretenses of bad men. Judas cared not for the poor—but he coveted that money. He did not see what good it could do to anoint the Lord with so very precious ointment. It was not necessary for purposes of health. And Mary might have honored Christ in some other way. Besides, by giving the price of that ointment to the Lord, who regarded the poor as his friends, and who always gave alms when he could, there would have been no waste. We have much Iscariot charity in our day. No doubt some said of Judas, "What a kind heart he has to the poor. He never forgets them." We have modern economists, who love Christ no more than Judas, and who extol everything that looks like saving money in efforts that are merely to honor Christ.

It is strange that the enemies of our Lord seem never to have thought of winning over any of his disciples. This is strong proof of the entire absence of suspicion respecting their fidelity. Accordingly they did not apply to any of the apostles to turn traitor; but "one of the twelve, called Judas Iscariot, went unto the chief priests, and said unto them, What will you give me, and I will deliver him unto you? And they covenanted with him for thirty pieces of silver. And from that time he sought opportunity to betray him." Matt. 26:14-16. This is the account given by one Evangelist. That of Luke is much like it, "Then Satan entered Judas, called Iscariot, who was numbered among the Twelve. He went away and discussed with the chief priests and temple police how he could hand Him over to them. They were glad and agreed to give him silver. So he accepted [the offer] and started looking for a good opportunity to betray Him to them when the crowd was not present." Luke 22:3-6. It is probable these enemies of Christ were much surprised when they saw

Judas, and still more when they learned his errand. This was the moment of exultation to wicked men and apostate angels. They seem to have thought that at last they would ease themselves of him whose sermons and miracles had made such an impression.

When Judas went to the chief priests, he probably expected to obtain several thousand pieces of silver, and thought thus to make his fortune. Possibly he intended to get his money, fulfill his bargain, and put his Master into their hands; and perhaps expected Christ immediately to deliver himself out of their power. Thus the traitor would have become a swindler. Whatever were his thoughts, he made the offer to betray him. The chief priests loved money, and understood bargaining. They probably saw in Judas an anxiety to hasten the matter. This would make them appear less careful in the business, until at length he sold to them the Lord of life and glory for thirty pieces of silver.

The bargain being made, the difficulty with Judas now was to fulfill his part of it. "And from that time he sought opportunity to betray him." Wickedness is troublesome. Probably Judas gave frequent assurances of fidelity in his covenant with the Jews, and would have pretended to be grossly insulted if any had charged him with a design of fraud. **Sin fearfully blinds the mind, and hardens the heart.** The devil seems now to have had full possession of Judas. He took no time—he had no heart for reflection. He may have kept up some form of prayer—but there was no sincerity in him or his devotions.

"At the celebration of the Passover, Jesus said, "While they were eating, He said, "I assure you: One of you will betray Me." Deeply distressed, each one began to say to Him, "Surely not I, Lord?" He replied, "The one who dipped his hand with Me in the bowl—he will betray Me. The Son of Man will go just as it is written about Him, but woe to that man by whom the Son of Man is betrayed! It would have been better for that man if he had not been born." Then Judas, His betrayer, replied, "Surely not I, Rabbi?" "You have said it," He told him." Matt. 26:21-25. When it is said they were "deeply distressed," the reference is doubtless to the others beside Judas. It almost broke their hearts to think it possible that they should prove traitors. But although Judas, last of all, asked, "Surely not I?" yet there is no evidence that he had any right feelings—but the contrary. As soon as Christ told him what he should do, Judas withdrew and sought his accomplices in wickedness.

This exposure before the whole family of Christ seems to have stirred up the deepest malice, and Judas felt no longer any restraint from the decencies of the case. The traitor having withdrawn, Jesus said, "Are you still sleeping and resting? Look, the time is near. The Son of Man is being betrayed into the hands of sinners. Get up; let's go! See—My betrayer is near. While He was still speaking, Judas, one of the Twelve, suddenly arrived. A large mob, with swords and clubs, was with him from the chief priests and elders of the people. His betrayer had given them a sign—The One I kiss, He's the One; arrest Him!" Matt. 26:45-49; compare Luke 22:47-49. What a band was this! What a betrayal was here! How cold and impudent the malignity of the traitor! How enormous his guilt! One would have expected that at this moment, hell would feel such mighty raven for her prey, as to open wide her mouth and swallow him alive. But his cup was not yet full. He who was ready to sell his Master, would soon be ready to throw himself away.

The deed was now done. The bargain was fulfilled on both sides. Judas had put his Master into the hands of his murderers, and he had obtained his promised reward. But presently the silver began to lose its luster, and the money its value. The price of blood began to torment its possessor. The inspired record is brief but striking, "Then Judas, His betrayer, seeing that He had been condemned, was full of remorse and returned the 30 pieces of silver to the chief priests and elders. "I have sinned by betraying innocent blood," he said. "What's that to us?" they said. "See to it yourself!" So he threw the silver into the sanctuary and departed. Then he went and hanged himself." Matt. 27:3-5. He could not endure the vicious gnaw of the undying worm. That silver filled his soul with intolerable horrors. Of late he had greatly desired it—but now he throws it down in the temple, and calls upon the priests, the ministers of religion, for some alleviation of his distress; but they are cold, and pay him no regard. They were not willing to receive back the price of his treason. Not believing in the value and efficacy of that blood which cleanses from all sin, not beholding in Jesus the Lamb of God who takes away the sin of the world, not finding any sympathy from his accomplices, conscience wielding over his guilty spirit the terrible sword of eternal and inflexible justice, and a hell burning within him, he hanged himself, jumped the awful gulf of death, and plunged into an undone eternity! "He went to his own place."

The aggravations of the sin of betraying Christ were many and great. The traitor was eminent in place, in gifts, in office, in profession; a guide to others, and one whose example was likely to influence many, and if evil, to give great occasion to the enemy to speak reproachfully. His sin had for its object the Lord Jesus Christ. It was an attack on God himself.

This sin admitted of no reparation, no restitution. It was against mercies, against convictions of conscience, against frequent and recent admonitions, against his ordination vows, against his own preaching, against all the rules of friendship, against all the bonds of discipleship. It was committed deliberately, willfully, knowingly, presumptuously, impudently, maliciously. It was perpetrated just after the most solemn and tender interview on record, just after being engaged in the most solemn rites of religion. It was of a scarlet dye and of a crimson hue.

Taking his own life was but adding iniquity to iniquity. He may have justified himself in his suicide, and thought that he had a right to do as he pleased with his earthly existence. Perhaps he thought also that hell itself could not be more intolerable than his present anguish. Miserable man! why will you place the seal of immutability on your own perdition, making your doom irreversible, and putting your soul beyond the reach of even the mercy of God? **Oh! what a fiend is man without the grace of God!** No natural amiability, no faithful instructions, no power of working miracles, no solemn sacraments, no tears and warnings can hold back any man from the vilest sins and the hottest hell. God's free, sovereign, eternal love can alone save any soul.

II. Let us note some of the principles which mark the providence of God towards this man.

1. All God does is just. In due time and manner, the Lord will show that he is righteous. His mercy may long be trampled on—but never with impunity. He is a jealous God, even when he seems for a season to let the wicked have their own way. God's character is safe in God's keeping. No man now dares to call in question the righteousness of the course of providence towards the son of perdition. The Judge of all the earth will do right; and he will make all the earth see it.

2. God often influences men by causes that seem to us very trivial. It is never safe to despise the day of small things, be they good or evil. Because God is almighty and all-wise, and man feeble and ignorant, mortals cannot tell whether an event or a cause is great or small. Little rills form the greatest rivers. The ocean itself is made up of drops of rain, or particles of mist. **A man is what his daily habits make him.** He who cannot resist a slight temptation is ill prepared to war with giants. "If racing against mere men

makes you tired, how will you race against horses? If you stumble and fall on open ground, what will you do in the thickets near the Jordan?" Jer. 12:5.

3. Providence so arranges human affairs that everything in life is a test of character. If one is rich, his wealth will try his humility. If one is poor, he will soon show whether he is contented. If a bribe is held out, it will evince how far covetousness prevails. If one is put into office like Judas, he himself may soon see whether his integrity is unspotted. If God leads the Israelites forty years through the wilderness, it is to humble them and to prove them. Deut. 8:2. If he feeds them with manna, it is for the same purpose. Deut. 8:16. If ambassadors are sent to Hezekiah, it is "to try him, that he might know all that was in his heart." 2 Chron. 32:31.

4. Such being the arrangements of providence it is impossible but that offences will come, as long as there are wicked men in the world. Luke 17:1. The wicked will do wickedly. Dan. 12:10. "There must also be heresies among you, that they which are approved may be made manifest among you." 1 Cor. 11:19. Open defections from truth and righteousness are to be expected in this wicked world. It has been so from the beginning. Jesus had his Judas; Peter, his Ananias; and Paul, his Demas. Those that are not of us, will go out from us. If they were of us, they would no doubt continue with us. The carnal and confident generally apostatize as soon as the heat of temptation is felt.

5. Providence so arranges affairs in this world, that even the wicked who hate him, shall certainly glorify him, even by their misdeeds. The treason of Judas was by the Lord overruled to bring about the most important event leading to man's salvation. Let the wicked never forget that their unbelief, impenitence, profaneness, and persecution of the godly, all their sins of heart, of life, and of tongue, shall in spite of themselves bring honor to God, though it be at the fearful loss of their own souls. The wicked now hate God but they cannot defeat him. If they will not be vessels to honor, they shall be vessels to dishonor. If they refuse to be useful in a cheerful service, they shall be useful in their own destruction. Ezek. 15:1-8; compare Psalm 76:10.

6. God will bring good out of evil, however atrocious it may be. This does not abate the guilt of those who work iniquity. There never was greater wickedness in any one act than in the treachery of Judas. Yet see what God has wrought thereby. His sin was foretold, and of course it was predetermined. Yet his accountability for his wickedness was unimpaired; for he acted freely in all

he did. Men may clamorously assert—but they never can prove that the divine purpose infracts human agency, or impairs human obligation. Judas could not have had more liberty; therefore his guilt remained. That which was true of the betrayer was also true of the murderers of our Lord. The same reasoning applies to both. Acts 2:23; 4:27, 28. "It is astonishing that men do not see that the whole system of prophecy is a direct and full confutation of all objections, against the doctrine of predestination. The predicted events cannot possibly fail of accomplishment; they must either therefore be absolutely decreed by the all-wise God, or there must be some necessity which cannot be overcome even by the Deity himself. The first is Christian predestination, the latter is heathen fatalism; but neither interferes with man's free agency or accountableness; for he still acts voluntarily, according to the prevailing inclinations of his heart."

7. So perfect is the providence of God over the hearts of all men that nothing is beyond his control. "The king's heart is in the hand of the Lord, as the rivers of water—he turns it wherever he will." Proverbs 21:1. Man cannot even have a thought that is not foolish and futile, unless as the Lord strengthens him. 2 Cor. 3:5.

8. Providence has so left things that the purest churches may have wicked members. The Lord has not granted the power of discerning spirits. Infallible evidence of love to Christ in our brethren is not attainable. A profession of piety accompanied by such evidence as an apparently consistent Christian life affords, is as much as we may demand. Our Lord knew Judas to be "a devil;" but his omniscience taught him this. Neither the profession nor outward life declared the baseness of the false disciple. So the Savior received him into the church, leaving us an example that we should follow his steps. Our Lord judged of the members of his church, not by what he as God knew of their hearts—but by their credible profession. He would not reject professors, who, in the judgment of charity, were honest. He practiced on the true rule. Let us seek no other. However painful our fears concerning the real characters of men, we must respect a credible profession of piety, not contradicted by a wicked life.

9. God has so arranged things that we ought to distinguish between personal and official character. If we do not, we will deceive, and be deceived. All official characters may be sustained without any real grace in the heart. Balaam's prophecies were as true and as sublime as those of Moses or of Isaiah. So far as we know, Judas' performance of the duties of his apostolic mission was as ac-

ceptable and as useful as that of a majority of his brethren. Even success in preaching is not proof of piety. It is the message, not the messenger; the truth preached, and not the man who utters it—which converts the soul. Piety is of infinite importance to every soul of man; but one who has no piety may yet do good. Neither the validity nor efficacy of ordinances depends upon the personal worthiness of the administrator. It would be very dangerous to teach that our acceptance in approaching God is rendered less certain by the hypocrisy of him who comes to us in Jehovah's name. The Apostles expressly denied that it was by their own power or holiness that they wrought miracles. The efficacy and saving power of ordinances are from the Lord alone. As worthy partakers of the Lord's Supper cannot be hindered by the insincerity of the administrator, so neither can the unworthy receiver secure the blessing by the piety of his minister.

10. The history of the world abounds with illustrations of this great principle in Providence—that however secret iniquity may be, it will ultimately find its way to the light. "Be sure your sin will find you out." Num. 32:23; compare 2 Sam. 12:12; Matt. 10:26; Mark 4:22; Luke 8:17; 12:2.

11. Sin kills the soul, and this according to the great laws of retribution. We see in Judas a fearful example of the terrible judgment of God against the wicked. As he loved cursing, so it came unto him—as he delighted not in blessing, so it was far from him. As he clothed himself with cursing like as with his garment, so it came into him like oil into his bones. Psalm 109:17, 18.

12. Every society of ungodly men has in it the elements of dissolution and of self-torment. There is no love between the wicked which can stand the test of severe trial. As sin is weakness, so, in his providence, God continually proves its hollowness and insufficiency to bind men together in concord and usefulness. As soon as the traitor's troubles came, his allies in sin cried, "What is that to us? See to that yourself." They never had any sympathy for him. They cruelly cast him off. Every sinner will at last esteem every other sinner and himself also a fool.

III. Such a history and such a course of providence teach us many things important for us all to learn. Let us not suppose that we are naturally better than Judas. Let us ponder the paths of our feet. Let us take heed to our ways, lest we also come to a bad end. The lessons we may learn are such as these—

When a man is once fairly started in a career of wickedness, it is impossible to tell where he will stop. God's grace may arrest one in the maddest career, as it did Saul of Tarsus. But left to himself, man will dig into hell. The good providence of God mercifully restrains even the wicked, else existence on earth would not be desirable. Scenes of violence and blood, deeds of outrage and atrocity, words of hatred and blasphemy, and looks of fierceness and terror would appall us every hour—but that God lays his almighty hand upon the hearts of men and commands them to be still. Unrestrained, every heart would show its possessor, to be a monster of wickedness. Passions, which now he smothered, would, if let loose, rage and sweep everything before them. Natural affection, the voice of conscience, public opinion, regard to reputation, and fear of the law, are happily employed by providence to hold men back. Even in this life many a poor sinner has been affrighted at the lengths which he had gone in crime and debasement, and has cried out in sore amazement, "And have I come to this?" In the next world astonishment awaits all the impenitent. "When they shall say, Peace and safety; then sudden destruction comes upon them, as travail upon a woman with child; and they shall not escape!" 1 Thess. 5:3.

All men should especially beware of covetousness. "The love of money is the root of all evil—which while some coveted after, they have erred from the faith, and pierced themselves through with many sorrows." 1 Tim. 6:10. Of the truth of this teaching Judas was a fearful witness. No tongue, no pen can describe the sorrows which rolled over his soul. When men are eagerly heaping up riches, they are doing work for bitter repentance in this world—or in that which is to come. Even on earth "the covetous man heaps up riches, not to enjoy them—but to have them; and starves himself in the midst of plenty; and most unnaturally cheats and robs himself of that which is his own; and is as poor and miserable with a great estate, as any man can be without it." Nor can he know who shall be the gainer by all his toils. "He heaps up riches, and knows not who shall gather them." Psalm 39:6. God has specially set himself to punish covetousness. It is idolatry. It is as true of this sin as of drunkenness, that in the end it bites like the serpent, and stings like the adder.

Did men but know how bitter would be the end of transgression, they would at least pause before they plunge into all evil. Seneca said, "Malice drinks half its own poison." The same is true of all evil passions. The madness of men in rebelling against God is beyond belief. They delight in iniquity, they roll it as a sweet morsel under their tongue, they risk all for it, and they lose all by it. Their hearts are fully set in them to do evil. Oh! that men would hear the warning words of Richard Baxter, "Use sin as it will use you; spare it not, for it will not spare you; it is your murderer and the murderer of the world. Use it, therefore, as a murderer should be used. Kill it before it kills you; and though it kills your bodies, it shall not be able to kill your souls; and though it brings you to the grave, as it did your Head, it shall not be able to keep you there." James says, "Sin, when it is finished, brings forth death." James 1:15. Yet **no man, without the grace of God, sees the evil of sin until it is too late.** Folly is bound up in the soul of man, until God drives it away by the beams of the Sun of Righteousness.

In Judas' pretended regard for the poor, we see what foul wickedness may be covered with the most plausible pretenses. The same thing is seen in every age. By false names every virtue is depressed, and every vice exalted. Pascal says, "One of the greatest artifices the devil uses to engage men in vice and debauchery, is to fasten the names of contempt on certain virtues, and thus to fill weak souls with a foolish fear of passing for scrupulous should they desire to put them in practice." The man who beggars widows and orphans, and holds back the wages of the hireling, and lives by the distresses he brings on others, would gladly persuade himself and his neighbors that he is prudent. Indeed, any pretext will satisfy a blind, stupid conscience. The great concern of the masses is to justify themselves before men. They little regard the tribunal of God. Yet the investigations of the last day will tear off all false pretenses, and sweep away every refuge of lies.

Nor should we forget that character may as well be learned from small things, as from great things. Judas' petty larceny was as good an index to his character as his treason. A straw will show which way the wind blows. Human character is not made up of a few great acts—but of a multitude of little things. **Every-day conduct shows the man.** Great events, in which we are actors, will fearfully expose us, if in small affairs we are unable to behave well. The failure of our virtue on great occasions is but an announcement to the world that we have been habitually coming short in our more private behavior.

It is also manifest that wicked men may for a long time appear well. To do so may cost them trouble—but may still be attainable. Through life they may have such a fear of exposure, and be so studious of appearances, as to deceive all around them. Suspicion may not even soil their fair name, and yet they may be in the gall of bitterness. Eschewing the vices of the debauched, they may practice the sins of devils. It is true that this class of transgressors have a hard task. They are always like one who has a rent in his garment, which he finds difficult to conceal. Truth is one and simple. Falsehood is multiform and complex. An honest blunderer is to be preferred before the most cunning knave on earth. A life of deception is full of hardship and uncertainty; and at its close, when amendment is impossible, the truth comes out, and in a moment damnation flashes in the face, and the poor soul enters on an existence full of misery. **When God tears away the mask, disguise is no longer possible!**

And yet bad men might know the truth concerning themselves if they did not hate it. Judas well knew his own theft, yet he refused to consider it a sin to be repented of. He had before his mind the clear evidence of his own hypocrisy—but he was not disposed to give it its just weight. He hated the light, and did not come to the light, lest his deeds should be reproved. When will men learn that concealment is not innocence? We may hide our sins from our own eyes—but until God casts them all behind his back they may rise up at any moment and overwhelm us. If men were not as unwise as they are wicked, they would not go to the bar of God with a lie in their right hand.

How small a temptation to sin will at last prevail over a wicked mind. For less than twenty dollars, Judas sold his Lord and Master. Those temptations commonly esteemed great, are not the most sure to prevail. The ribaldry of the Philistines did not move Samson from his fidelity; but the blandishments of Delilah overcame him. Esau sold his birthright for a bowl of soup. Many a man consents to lose his soul for a quibble. **Men may sin until the mere force of habit, without any apparent inducement, seems sufficient to impel them to great enormities.**

Nothing prepares a man for destruction faster than hypocrisy or formality, in actions of a religious nature. The three years which Judas spent in the family of our Lord probably exceeded all the rest of his life in ripening him for destruction. So many, so solemn, so impressive truths were presented to his mind, that he must have become very rapidly hardened. "I have peace-offerings with me; this day have I paid my vows," Proverbs 7:14, said one who was now ready for the worst deeds. The reason why, other things being equal, apostates are so much more wicked than others, is that they have learned how to resist all good influences. They have tried the remedy—but first learned to render it ineffectual.

It is a small matter to be judged of man's judgment. The judgment of God, it shall stand—it is righteous, it is always according to truth. **Man judges of the heart by appearances. God judges of appearances by the heart**, and he judges of the heart by itself. The tribunal, from which there lies no appeal, will reverse a vast number of the decisions made by the tribunals of earth. Public opinion often errs. Individual judgments are as often erroneous. If men condemn and God approves—all is well. But if men acquit and God condemns—all is lost. He who judges us is the Lord.

The history of Judas shows us how man will cling to false hopes. Hypocrites hold fast their delusive expectations with the utmost tenacity. There is no evidence that during years of hypocrisy Judas ever seriously doubted his own piety. There were many sure marks, indeed, against him; but what does any hypocrite care for such evidence? His own blind confidence is to him more powerful than all the truths of God's word. Because he is determined to believe his state to be good, nothing will convince him to the contrary.

We have a full refutation of the objection made to a connection with the visible church, because there are wicked men in her communion. The apostles certainly knew that among them was one wicked man; but they did not therefore renounce their portion among Christ's confessed friends. And Christ himself held fellowship with Judas just as if he were all he professed to be. So that if one certainly knew another to be an enemy of God, and yet could not prove it to the satisfaction of impartial church authorities, this should not debar him from the Lord's table. If dogs will sometimes get the children's bread, that is no reason why a table should not be spread for the children.

In all our dealings with men, it is better to be sometimes imposed on, than to be of a suspicious temper. "With what judgment you judge, you shall be judged." Sometimes we must put ourselves in the power of others. To suspect every man will make us unhappy, and commonly prove us to be unworthy of confidence ourselves. Even a wise man of the world once said, "Always to think the worst, I have ever found to be the mark of a base spirit."

How difficult it is to bring home truth to the deceitful heart of man. Hypocrites are slow to improve close, discriminating preaching. They desire not to look into their real characters. It was not until all the rest had inquired whether Christ referred to them in foretelling his betrayal, that Judas said, "Lord, is it I?" Thorough, impartial, frequent self-examination is not the characteristic of any who are at heart unsound. In fact, the reluctance of some to this duty is sad evidence against them. It costs them too much. Aversion to close, searching sermons is a bad mark in any man's character. Such preaching often afflicts the righteous more than the wicked, though the latter are the most apt to be offended. When Christ had exposed the miserable hypocrisy of many who followed him, it is said, "From that time many of his disciples went back, and walked no more with him." John 6:66. They could not endure the truth. Yet Judas smothered up his feelings, and bore it all. He cared not so much for his feelings. He went after his covetousness.

Nor could one do a wiser thing than to inquire whether he has better evidence of piety than the great traitor had during his apostleship. Judas could heal the sick, raise the dead, and cast out demons. He was first a disciple, and then an apostle of our Lord. He often heard Christ preach. He held the only office of trust among the apostles—the treasurer. His reputation for piety stood as fair as any man's. His persuasion of his good state seems to have been so firm, that he hardly felt inclined to look into the grounds of his hopes. He was not a drunkard, nor a swearer. He was not a faultfinding hearer of the Gospel. Without a murmur he bore all the fatigue of his apostolic mission. He was not an envious man beyond others. He was not a slanderer, a reviler, a backbiter, a whisperer. He displayed no inordinate ambition. He was not a brawler, nor a violent and outrageous man. And yet he was not a child of God. Mere negative goodness, mere freedom from open vice—proves no man an heir of glory. It is true there was sufficient evidence against Judas—but he willingly overlooked that. If many men had as good evidence against their enemies or their neighbors, as they have against themselves, they would speedily pronounce them hypocrites.

The case of Judas discloses the uselessness of that *sorrow of the world* which works death, has no hope in it, and drives the soul to madness. It is not desperation—but penitence, that God requires. Regrets without hatred of sin are useless, both on earth and in hell. They avail nothing in time, nothing in eternity. When it is said Judas repented, the word translated, *repented*, is not the word used by inspired writers to express godly sorrow, or saving repentance. There is much sorrow that does but prepare men for other and more dreadful deeds.

God's judgments are still abroad in the earth. Of all judgments, those which are spiritual should most alarm us. To have eyes and not see, to have ears and not hear, to have hearts and not understand, to hold the truth in unrighteousness, to be forsaken of God, to be given over to believe a lie—these are among the direst curses that fall on men in this world and they are sure forerunners of God's sorest plagues in the world to come. And how fearful must it be to fall into the hands of the living God, when on earth a drop of his wrath will make men choose hanging rather than life. And how dismal must be the prospects of all who die in their sins, when they shall have for their companions Judas and all evil-minded men, the devil and his angels. The society of the damned, is great incentive for earnestly fleeing from the wrath to come.

The doctrine of universal salvation has no warrant in Scripture. It is disproven by many express declarations, and by many fair and necessary inferences. It is disproven by the case of Judas. If, after many thousand years of suffering, he shall rise to everlasting happiness in the skies, it will be good for him that he was born. Eternal happiness far outweighs all temporal suffering, however protracted. Any existence which terminates in eternal glory will prove a blessing beyond all computation. All temporal suffering can be gauged. But who can fathom the sea of love, the ocean of bliss, made sure to all believers? And eternal misery is as dreadful—as eternal glory is delightful. Oh! how fearful must be the doom of the incorrigibly wicked, when in their case existence itself ceases to be desirable, or even tolerable! It is true of everyone who dies without repentance toward God, and faith in our Lord Jesus Christ, that it had been good for that man if he had not been born. "Woe to that man by whom the Son of Man is betrayed! It would have been better for that man if he had not been born." Matthew 26:24

THE MYSTERIES OF GOD'S PROVIDENCE

"When I tried to understand all this, it was oppressive to me." Psalm 73:16

Providence is a greater mystery than revelation. The state of the world is more humiliating to our reason than the doctrines of the gospel. A reflecting Christian sees more to excite his astonishment, and to exercise his faith, in the state of things in this world—than in what he reads from Genesis to Revelation. (Cecil.)

God act according to rules of wisdom and justice, which it may be quite impossible by our faculties to apprehend, or understand. (Barrow.)

There is, and ever was somewhat, very much, in God's providential administration of the things of this world, which the most improved reason of men cannot reach unto, and which is contrary to all that is in us, as merely men. (John Owen.)

The book of Providence is inextricable and unintelligible to the wisest of men, who are not governed by the word of God. But when the principles of Scripture are admitted and understood, they throw a pleasing light upon the study of Divine Providence, and at the same time are confirmed and illustrated by it. (John Newton.)

As the heavens are higher than the earth, so are my ways higher than your ways, and my thoughts than your thoughts. (Jehovah.)

No subject has more perplexed godly men, than the dark aspects of Providence. Jeremiah was humble and very tender-hearted, yet he says, "Why are the wicked so prosperous? Why are evil people so happy?" This pious, humble servant of God was sore perplexed. Indeed the Scriptures everywhere admit that God's ways are unsearchable. "Your judgments are a great deep." Psalm 36:6. "Your way is in the sea, and your path in the great waters, and your footsteps are not known." Psalm 77:19. "Marvelous are your works." Psalm 139:14. Even in heaven itself; glorified ones sing, "Great and marvelous are your works, Lord God Almighty." Rev. 15:3. So that inspiration itself everywhere covers the eternal throne with clouds and darkness, and admits that acts of providence are veiled in mystery. Wonders will never cease. Heaven is full of mysteries, though none of them are painful—but all of them glorious.

Let us look at several things which must ever make the providence of God mysterious to pious men in this world.

1. God's ways of working are infinitely diversified, even in the midst of a general uniformity. He saves or he destroys in any way he pleases, by the strong, or by the weak; by friend or by foe; when danger is seen, and when it is unseen. He sends an army of men, or an army of caterpillars to punish a guilty nation. In either case the work is done. He shakes a leaf, or sends an earthquake, and each does its errand. God is confined to no routine. He knows and commands all causes, all agents, all truths, all errors, all influences, and all oppositions. At a nod he makes the great, small; or the small, great. No mortal can tell which of two causes is the greater, until he sees what God will make of them. Men and causes are considerable or contemptible according to the fiat of Jehovah. That which to us sometimes seems like confusion, is in fact all order.

In the seventy-third Psalm, Asaph tells us at length of his deep and terrible perplexity when looking at the ways of God. Coming to a knowledge of his own ignorance, and of the infinite glory of God, his troubles vanish; and he concludes his sorrowful meditations with the exultant assurance, "Whom have I in heaven but you? and there is none upon earth that I desire beside you. My flesh and my heart fails—but God is the strength of my heart and my portion forever."

2. For many things in providence we can give no account, except that so it seemed good to the Judge of all the earth. Who can tell why bloody Nero was left to ruin by his passions, and Saul of Tarsus, no less bloody, was saved? Why was repentance granted to one thief on the cross, while the other died a blasphemer? The mercies received by any man are wholly undeserved. No man merits any good thing at the hand of his Maker. Yet all receive many mercies, and some are blessed with all spiritual blessings in Christ Jesus. On the other hand, why is one man more afflicted than another? All our afflictions are deserved, yes, they are always fewer than we deserve. Indeed the wonder is we suffer so little. But the whole doctrine of divine judgments is of difficult interpretation, when we come to individual cases.

McCosh says, "It is comparatively seldom that we have such a minute acquaintance with every event in the past life of a neighbor, as to be able to determine the precise end contemplated in any visitation of God towards him. In some cases, indeed, the connection is manifest to the man's intimate friend, or to the world at large, as when intemperance and excess lead to poverty and disease, and cunning leads to distrust, and is caught in the net which it laid for others. In other cases, the connection is only visible to the individual himself, or his most intimate friends. In all cases, it is easier to determine the meaning of the judgments of God in reference to ourselves, than in their reference to others, when they are exposed to them. Being ourselves acquainted with all the incidents of our past life, we may trace a connection between deeds which we have done, and trials sent upon us—a connection which no other is intended to perceive, or so much as to suspect. While affliction can in no case prove the existence of sin not otherwise established, yet it may be the means of leading the person afflicted to inquire; whether he may not in his past life have committed some sin, of which this is the punishment or cure. Here, as in many other cases, the rule is to be strict in judging ourselves and slow in judging others."

3. The absence of pomp and parade in God's providence, has struck many. How noiseless are most of his doings. When in spring Jehovah would reanimate all nature, bring into activity myriads of insects, give growth to millions of seeds, and clothe mountains and valleys in living green—it is all a silent work.

When he would subvert a universal monarchy, long before the time set for that purpose, he puts it into the heart of a great ruler to build a bridge, and for that purpose to change the channel of a river for a season. This is all done without signs in heaven, or war in the elements. In the fullness of time the same river is, by means the simplest, diverted from its channel. Belshazzar is slain, Babylon is a prey to the invader, and a universal empire is dissolved.

Commonly when God depopulates cities and kingdoms, his messengers pass silently along, and do their work before men are aware. There was no noise of preparation for the destruction of Sodom and Gomorrah. The morning of their eternal overthrow was as calm as any on which the sun had risen upon them. The destroying angel, who slew the first-born of Egypt, spread his mighty wings over the land, and from them dropped down death on every habitation of man and beast. Yet all was quiet as the grave, until the wail of bereavement filled the land with terror.

God makes a world with less noise than that produced by man when he makes a coffin. When Jehovah spread out the heavens and set up their unshaken pillars, there was not so much as the sound of a hammer. When on our best railroads we travel at the rate of sixty miles an hour, the rumbling noise is heard afar, the sight of our speed is startling to every spectator, and we cannot divest ourselves of apprehension. But ever since we were born we have been riding on a world moved by God at the rate of more than sixty-two thousand miles every hour. And yet who has been afraid? Who has heard any startling sound? This is the more wonderful because the motion of the earth is not simple, but complex. Yet in the midst of all this speed we can hear the chirping of a bird, or the dropping of a pin. But when God chooses, he can make our ears to tingle. By the shaking of a leaf he can startle us, or make us rise up with alarming sounds. "The thunder of his power who can understand?" When he shall destroy the world it shall be with sounds that shall awake the dead. "The heavens shall pass away with a great noise." When God chooses to be heard, even the mountains give ear and obey his voice. At his rebuke he dries up the sea, and makes the river a wilderness. Yet, ordinarily, his footsteps are not heard, and **his voice is but the silent going forth of his almighty energy**.

4. In his mysterious providence God also hides his works and ways from man by commonly removing results far from human view. In autumn the farmer scatters his wheat and buries it under the ground. It dies. Search and you shall find it rotten. The rigors of a long winter are approaching. The unskilled would say this sowing of seed was madness. It was casting bread upon the waters. But wait until summer, and that farmer shall shout his *harvest home*. What thus occurs in the natural world is a type of spiritual things. "They who sow in tears shall reap in joy. He who goes forth and weeps, bearing precious seed, shall doubtless come again with rejoicing, bringing his sheaves with him." Much as the blessed result is hoped for, it is not perceived by any mortal. None but God sees the end from the beginning. Whom he would bless, he first puts to the test of patient waiting. **If the righteous should see the happy outcome of all that befalls them—as it lies open before God—their afflictions would be no trials.** Had Abraham known that all God would require of him would be to bind Isaac and lay him on the altar, we never would have heard of the illustrious faith of the father of believers. Jacob once cried out, "Joseph is not, and Simeon is not, and you will take Benjamin away. All these things are **against** me!" He lived to see that all these things were **for** him. But at the time of his bereavement he saw not the blessed end, and so his virtue was severely tested.

If on the day of crucifixion, as on the day of Pentecost, the disciples had clearly perceived the results of that scene of terror, the Shepherd might have been smitten—but the sheep would hardly have been scattered. And it is as true of the wicked as of the righteous—that they cannot foresee results; they cannot tell what God is about to do. None are more surprised than the wicked at the conclusion of things under God's control. The sinner intends—but God superintends. The creature appoints—but God disappoints. Man proposes—but God disposes. Lazarus was filled with wonder to find himself in Abraham's bosom—but Dives was sorely amazed to find himself in hell. Neither Pharaoh, nor Belshazzar, nor Herod, nor Pilate, expected such results to themselves as their wickedness wrought out. "Sin, when it is finished, brings forth death." The wicked have the hope of heaven, in the midst of all iniquity and unbelief. How sorely will their souls be vexed when they find themselves eternally, hopelessly disappointed.

5. God's ways respecting means are very remarkable. So far as we can see, he often works without means. Perceiving no causes in operation, we expect no effects. Seeing no disease, we expect no death. Not perceiving any cause for a certain trial—it finds us unprovided with remedies, and we are ready to be swallowed up. As we begin to give up all hope, God steps in and relieves us. When he chooses, he dispenses with all means. He did so when he made the world. He has often done so since. "I will have mercy upon the house of Judah, and will save them by the Lord their God, and will not save them by bow nor by sword, nor by battle, nor by horses, nor by horsemen." Hos. 1:7.

Again, **God often works by means, which seem to us INSIGNIFICANT**. Burke, "The death of a man at a critical juncture, his disgust, his retreat, his disgrace—have brought innumerable evils on a whole nation. A common soldier, a child, a girl at the door of an inn—have changed the face of fortune, and almost the face of nature." Wellington, "The stumbling of a horse may decide the outcome of a battle—and so the destinies of an empire!" Will God save Rome from pillage? It shall be done by the cackling of geese. Has a man's appointed time upon earth expired? The sting of a bee, the scratch of a pin, a crumb of bread, or a spring zephyr—shall be the means of his death! Will God prolong the life of Hezekiah? A lump of figs shall have healing efficacy. Will he raise up a wonderful nation? It shall be from a man, whose body was dead, he being about a hundred years old, and the womb of his wife dead also. Rom. 4:19.

Moreover **God often works CONTRARY to means**. How much

bad practice in medicine does he provide against, and thus restore the patient! How many blunders in his ministers does he overrule for good! Christ would give sight to a blind man. He makes clay, puts it on his eyes as if to make him more blind—but he is healed. A terrible fall dislocates a joint. The bone is not put rightly back into its place. Years of lameness and suffering follow. A second fall, worse than the first, jars the frame, jeopardizes life—but restores the bone to its socket, and soon the man walks and leaps and praises God. By death, God destroyed him that had the power of death. God often works contrary to the natural tendency of means.

5. God also employs such instruments as greatly confound us. Our ignorance and unbelief would choose those instruments which God rejects; and reject those instruments which he selects. Will he cure Naaman's leprosy? A little captive maid shall tell him of the prophet of the Lord. Will he lead forth Israel from Egyptian bondage? That little infant in a basket among the reeds, by edict doomed to death as soon as born, shall be the deliverer. Will he make Joseph prime minister of Egypt? His brethren envy and sell him, the Ishmaelites carry him far from all loved ones, Potiphar imprisons him, the iron enters into his flesh; yet in God's providence every step is ordained to the destined result.

How often are those whom we never befriended made to minister to our aid and comfort! Must God's people be brought out of Babylon? Cyrus shall send forth the binding decree. This worshiper of the sun deals as tenderly with God's people as a nurse with her child. It would not have been more wonderful to see the wolf nourishing and protecting a lamb. Who would have supposed that God would choose a raven to feed Elijah, the boy Samuel to bear heavy tidings to Eli, or the youth Jeremiah to pull down, destroy and build up kingdoms? God would exalt his Son and give him a name, which is above every name. He is made flesh, born in a manger, is subject to his parents, is tempted, mocked, spit upon, betrayed, denied, condemned, crucified, dead and buried—yet all ends in his exaltation. He, who made swaddling bands for the sea, was laid in swaddling clothes, that he might be the first-born among many brethren. By falling he arose above all his enemies, above all the creatures of God.

Will God bring the gospel to the ends of the world? It shall not be done by the ministry of angels—but to the poor, condemned, and dying—the riches of his mercy shall be borne in earthen vessels. Will God subdue the world to knowledge, to peace and righteousness? Humble men shall be his ambassadors. Will he make of his people a glorious church? "Brothers, consider your calling: not many are wise from a human perspective, not many powerful, not many of noble birth. Instead, God has chosen the world's foolish things to shame the wise, and God has chosen the world's weak things to shame the strong. God has chosen the world's insignificant and despised things—the things viewed as nothing—so He might bring to nothing the things that are viewed as something, so that no one can boast in His presence." 1 Corinthians 1:26-29

Look at that godly man surrounded by an infuriated throng. Each one gnashes with his teeth and is intense for his prey. At the giving of the signal, stone follows stone. Gash after gash is made on the body of the pious sufferer. The blood streams from his head and body. Nearby him stands a small young man, drinking in with malignant joy the groans that fall from the martyr's lips. Like a young tiger, hitherto fed on milk—but now tasting blood, he becomes furious against all who call on the name of Jesus. He breathes out threatenings and slaughter. He sheds innocent blood without remorse and without cessation. Who would believe that this persecutor was the chosen of God, and should yet, with unparalleled zeal and incredible success, preach Jesus, call sinners to repentance, and give joy and courage to the trembling disciples? Yet such was God's plan—and it was all executed.

God is a sovereign. His counsel shall stand. He will do all his pleasure. He rejected all the seven elder sons of Jesse, and chose the little boy, David, who had been left with the sheep, and made him king of his people, and the sweet singer of Israel. "Man looks on the outward appearance—but the Lord looks on the heart." Most of the great, useful, and honored men of the next generation are now poor boys, unnoticed by the proud, buffeting difficulties, and forming vigorous characters under the influence of neglect and adversity. Matthew Henry says, "The most splendid women the world ever saw, have been those who were most familiar with toil and care."

7. We often tremble to see God pursuing a course which, to our short sight, seems quite contrary to the end to be gained. This is for two purposes. The first is to humble us and thus prepare us for the reception of his great blessings. The other is to prove that "besides him there is no Savior." When mountains and waters and cruel Egyptians hedged in the Israelites on every side, and it was manifest that "in vain was the help of man!" Then came the word, "Stand still and see the salvation of God," and the sea was cleft in two, and its waves became walls. "In the mount it shall be seen" is for a saying in Israel. Even the gospel was not sent until men had racked their inventions, and were at their wit's end. "For since in the wisdom of God the world through its wisdom did not know him, God was pleased through the foolishness of what was preached to save those who believe." Everything in its order. When wit has shown its weakness—then God's word comes in, and speaks wisdom. When human powers fall prostrate, divine energy produces the desired results.

The mysteries of providence are very vast. No created mind can fathom them. Let us dwell on the subject a little further, in the order already observed.

8. Men are so ignorant of their own hearts that they are incapable of determining what is best for them. Even regenerate men are but partially sanctified and enlightened. But God searches the heart. He understands our whole case. He knows what is most for our good. He sees our strong corruptions and sad deficiencies. When, in mercy to His child, he comes to heal his spiritual maladies, he does not take counsel with human reasoning or desires. It is right, it is best that he should act according to the wisdom which is infallible. He employs the requisite remedies. Often they are distasteful to flesh and blood. Sometimes they are frightful to contemplate and terrible to endure. Then man, in his ignorance, too often says, "If God loved me, he would not give me so bitter a cup to drink!" But this is man's folly. Shall not the Judge of all the earth do right? Shall human weakness control divine power? Shall finite knowledge prescribe to omniscience? It is the height of wickedness for a worm of the dust to revise the decisions, or pre-judge the justice of the Almighty. We should expect that God would deal with us, in an incomprehensible way—if we did but remember how base, sordid, and narrow are our views and plans; and how holy, glorious, and eternal are his purposes and designs. We are quite prone to magnify both the good and evil things of time, to the disparagement of those of eternity. But when God thwarts, afflicts, and mortifies us—he makes us look at the things which are unseen and eternal. If he racks this body with pain, it is that we may think of our house, not made with hands, eternal, and in the heavens. The shaking of this clay tabernacle forces upon us the recollection that this is not our rest, and that we ought to be seeking a heavenly country. If the godliest man on earth had his own way without divine guidance—he would soon be in full march towards destruction!

How kind is God in wisely and mercifully deciding so many things for us! The man who fears God and loves his little daughter, would esteem it a greater affliction to be called on to say *when* his child should be sick—than he now finds it to nurse her through weeks of disease, close her eyes in death, and then carry her to the grave. God very mercifully bears the heaviest part of all our trials, by marking out our course for us. God is governor. We are servants. To us belong obedience, submission, acquiescence. It is not ours to guide, to decide what is best, to rule the world, to shape the course of events.

9. It is very remarkable that God so strangely upholds his people, and keeps them from falling into sin. How often are their feet ready to slip—and yet how commonly are they upheld. The wonder is that they do not fall every day. But the promise even concerning the weak among them is that they shall be held up, for God is able to make them stand. True, his grace is secretly supplied, and that is their support. But his providence often hedges them about, surrounds them with motives to right conduct, sends seasonable hints and warnings, points out the wretchedness of transgression, and so holds them up. "The deliverances of God's people," says Flavel, "are often as remote from their expectations, as from the designs of their enemies." "Hold me up, and I shall be safe!" Psalm 119:117

10. To some God's providence is full of mystery, because at times he works so slowly, and at other times he works so rapidly. Sometimes he takes scores and even hundreds of years to effect a purpose. Again he cuts short the work in righteousness. From the day that Joseph is sold to the Ishmaelites until he and his brethren are reconciled are four and twenty long years, while in less than twenty-four hours, Daniel is delivered from the lions' den and from the fearful conspiracy against him. The Babylonish captivity lasts seventy years, and yet probably in less than seventy minutes, Shadrach, Meshach and Abednego are brought out of the burning fiery furnace unhurt. "My times are with you, O God." God takes his own time and is never in a hurry, and is never slack as some men account these things. One day is with the Lord as a thousand years and a thousand years as one day.

11. Hardly anything in Providence is more incomprehensible than the lengths to which God often permits men to go in the way of transgression before he brings them to a saving knowledge of Christ Jesus. Yonder goes a funeral procession. A large and respectable church is burying one of its most valued members. He has lately departed this life in the triumphs of faith.

His death was preceded by months of painful sickness, which was borne with sweet submission to God's will. This sickness was preceded by more than a dozen years of close, humble walking with God, as the fruit of a clear conversion. But that conversion was preceded by more than a dozen years of shocking intemperance and profaneness, during which promises were made, pledges given, and oaths taken that the cup of poison should be laid aside—but all in vain. A voyage to sea was alike ineffectual. So desperate was that man's state of mind that he often said, "If I could see the world wrapped in flames, I would clap my hands for joy." At length he determined on self-destruction. The deadly poison is procured. The vial is emptied—but the stomach refuses to retain it. Life is prolonged. At last he resolves to pray for strength to overcome his dreadful sin. His prayer is heard. This leads him to pray for other things. The result is his salvation.

Nor was this a solitary case. Some of the converted members of the church at Corinth had been sexually immoral people, idolaters, adulterers, male prostitutes, homosexuals, thieves, greedy people, drunkards, revilers, or swindlers. Nor were they the only ones, whose state was debased before their conversion. The whole church at Ephesus was made up of those who had been "once darkness," but by their happy change were now "light in the Lord." In countries but recently enlightened by the Gospel are found in the churches many, who once sacrificed their children to devils.

12. Four things in God's providential dealings which we are not able to grapple with. (From John Owen)

1. Visible confusion. The oppression of tyrants, wasting of nations, destruction of men and animals, fury and desolations—make up the things of the past and present ages. Also, the greatest and choicest parts of the earth, in the meantime are inhabited by those who know not God, who hate him, who fill and replenish the world with habitations of cruelty, sporting themselves in mischief, like the leviathan in the sea, etc.

2. Unspeakable variety. Instance the case of the saints. In what unspeakable variety are they dealt with! Some under persecution always, some always at peace, some in dungeons and prisons, some at liberty in their own houses; the saints of one nation under great oppression for many ages, of another in quietness; in the same places some poor, in great distress, and put hard to it to gain their bread all their lives; others abounding in all things; some full of various afflictions, going softly and mourning all their days; others spared and scarce touched with the rod at all; and yet commonly the advantage of holiness, and close walking with God, lying on the distressed side, etc.

3. Sudden alterations. As in the case of Job, God takes a man who was blessed with choice blessings, in the midst of a course of obedience and close walking with himself, when he expected to die in his nest, and to see good all his days—ruins him in a moment; blasts his name, that he who was esteemed a choice saint, shall not be able to deliver himself from the common esteem of the hypocrite; slays his children; takes away his rest, health, and everything that is desirable to him. This amazes the soul, it knows not what God is doing, nor why he pleads with it in so much bitterness, etc.

4. Great, deep, and abiding distresses have the same effects, etc.

13. Nothing in providence is more inscrutable than the ever new discoveries and evolutions of the grace and wisdom of God towards his people. "He who spared not his own Son—but delivered him up for us all, how shall he not with him also freely give us all things?" Romans 8:32. In one of his epistles (Titus 3:4) Paul speaks of the *philanthropy* of God, in the English properly rendered, *love toward man.* "After that the kindness and love of God toward man appeared," etc. The same word occurs in the New Testament but in one other place, Acts 28:2, where it is said, "The barbarous people showed us no little *kindness.*" Their philanthropy consisted in kindling a fire and in hospitably receiving each of the sufferers from the rain and cold.

If such philanthropy as this is worthy of mention in the Book of God, surely the philanthropy of Jehovah in rescuing sinners from everlasting misery by the gift of his Son should never be forgotten while eternity endures. The Bible tells us that God's love is from everlasting to everlasting, that it is vastly productive of glory to God and salvation to man, that it is wholly gracious—but it never claims to do the subject justice. Jesus himself says, "God so loved the world," John 3:16, and the beloved disciple exclaims, "Behold what manner of love." 1 John 3:1. But neither the Master nor the beloved disciple can tell us the full meaning of the word, *so*, or of the phrase, *what manner.* The love of no mother is equal to the love of the Savior, Isaiah 49:15, and its developments and evolutions will be more and more glorious forever and ever.

14. Nor is all this strange if we duly consider that—God's providence is the acting out of his infinite perfections. Neither man nor angel comprehends the infinitude of his resources, the infallibility of his truth, the glory of his holiness, the power of his wrath, the fearfulness of his praises. He works like a God. His whole plans are on a scale so entirely above the comprehension of creatures, that angels no less than pious men, wonder and worship.

15. Nor can any creature ever make straight that which is crooked, nor smooth that which is rough, nor light that which is dark. Who can comprehend the inequality of the circumstances of mortals? Why are some men poor—while others no more virtuous are rich? Why are some feeble—while others are strong? Why are some unfortunate in almost every enterprise—while others hardly touch anything that does not seem to enhance their earthly comfort? Job saw these things, "The tents of robbers are safe, and those who provoke God are secure. Which of all these does not know that the hand of the Lord has done this? The life of every living thing is in His hand, as well as the breath of all mankind."

16. Another thing that must invest the providence of God with perpetual mystery to mortals is the fact that all the mightiest agencies in the universe are invisible. No man has seen God at any time. No man can see his face and live. "When he passes me, I cannot see him; when he goes by, I cannot perceive him." "But if I go to the east, he is not there; if I go to the west, I do not find him.

9 When he is at work in the north, I do not see him; when he turns to the south, I catch no glimpse of him." Job 9:11; 23:8, 9. So likewise the agency of angels has almost always been beyond our perception, except by its effects. They excel in strength. One of them destroyed an army of one hundred and eighty-five thousand men in one night. Yet no one perceived him. In like manner, the evil influence of fallen angels is not observed. Thus the whole power of thrones, dominions and principalities pertaining to the invisible world eludes the grasp of our senses; yet nothing to an equal extent operates on this world.

"Wisdom and strength belong to God; counsel and understanding are His. Whatever He tears down cannot be rebuilt; whoever He imprisons cannot be released. When He withholds the waters, everything dries up, and when He releases them, they destroy the land. True wisdom and power belong to Him. The deceived and the deceiver are His. He leads counselors away barefoot and makes judges go mad. He releases the bonds put on by kings and ties a cloth around their waists. He leads priests away barefoot and overthrows established leaders. He deprives trusted advisers of speech and takes away the elders' good judgment. He pours out contempt on nobles and disarms the strong. He reveals mysteries from the darkness and brings the deepest darkness into the light. He makes nations great, then destroys them; He enlarges nations, then leads them away. He deprives the world's leaders of reason, and makes them wander in a trackless wasteland. They grope around in darkness without light—He makes them stagger like drunken men." Job 12:13-25 These are but a few of the just and sublime statements of the man of Uz, respecting the undeniable mysteries connected with the invisible agency of the Lord Almighty.

PRACTICAL REMARKS ON THE MYSTERIES OF GOD'S PROVIDENCE

I. Let not the wicked infer that a change will never come. Among some of the ancients, the emblem of justice was an old man, strong but lame, with a sharp sword, proceeding slowly to his work. "May the Lord bring their flattery to an end and silence their proud tongues. They say, "We will lie to our hearts' content. Our lips are our own—who can stop us?" The Lord replies, "I have seen violence done to the helpless, and I have heard the groans of the poor. Now I will rise up to rescue them, as they have longed for me to do." Psalm 12:3-5. The Lord will not always chide his people, neither will he always let the wicked go unpunished. He sees that their day is coming. The wonder is that they do not see it also.

II. Let us not judge the Lord at all, but let us judge this—that we are very ignorant and foolish, and that if we would be wise, we must listen, and study, and learn our lessons from the infallible Teacher. If we will not be candid and diligent students of God's word and providence, we must live and die without wisdom. Oh that every man knew that he himself is a fool—and that Jehovah alone is God. We are indeed poor judges of what is best. We cannot see afar off. Not a single event of Providence is completed. We know but in part. How can we competently decide upon the whole by the little fragments we possess? An axe by itself, and the saw by itself, are alike useless to the woodman; but properly unite them, and the monarch of the forest soon bows his majestic head before him who wields this little instrument. Man's glory is not the ultimate end of any of the divine proceedings. All things are made for the pleasure and the glory of him who has called us into being, and governs us with his almighty hand.

III. Let us possess our souls in patience. Were we required to govern the world with our present darkness of mind, we might well despair. But as our duty is not to rule but to submit. What we need is a quiet mind to stand and adoringly view the majesty and government of him who works all things after the counsel of his own will. **Promises** do you need? Here they are—

"As your days, so shall your strength be."

"Trust in the Lord, and do good; so shall you dwell in the land, and verily you shall be fed."

"Delight yourself also in the Lord, and he shall give you the desires of your heart."

"Commit your way unto the Lord; trust also in him, and he shall bring it to pass."

"Rest in the Lord, and wait patiently for him."

"I will make you my wife forever, showing you righteousness and justice, unfailing love and compassion. I will be faithful to you and make you mine."

"I will allure her, and bring her into the wilderness, and speak comfortably unto her."

"I will be as the dew unto Israel."

"The eternal God is your refuge, and underneath are the everlasting arms."

Lean on these promises—and hope to the end.

IV. Let us rejoice in hope of God's glory. It is coming. It is surely coming. All the combinations of the wicked cannot hinder it. We shall see it, only let us believe. We may shout the victor's song, even here. God shall be glorified, and we shall see him honored. If we are truly his, we shall be honored with him. Come, O long-expected Deliverer, come to be admired in all your saints. Pious soul, do you need encouragement to hope? You have it, "Fear not those things, which you shall suffer." "He who endures to the end—shall be saved." "Father, I will that they whom you have given me, be with me that they may behold my glory." O pilgrim of the narrow way! Rejoice, for your redemption draws near.

V. Let us never arrogantly claim to understand the counsels of the Most High God. "As the heavens are higher than the earth, so are God's ways higher than our ways, and God's thoughts than our thoughts." "The secret things belong to the Lord our God." Clearly the finite can never comprehend the infinite. Yet,

VI. Let us study and observe the ways of the Almighty. "Who is wise? He will realize these things. Who is discerning? He will understand them. The ways of the Lord are right; the righteous walk in them, but the rebellious stumble in them." Hosea 14:9. Though we cannot grasp the heavens, yet we may look up to them, and see some of the wonders they reveal, and learn at least our own nothingness. "The fainter our light is, the more intent we should be in looking; the knottier the subject, the more earnest should be our study on it." Yet as a jury, in a criminal cause, may receive impressions in the progress of the trial—but should feel bound to suspend judgment until the whole facts of the case are submitted; so nothing can warrant us in pronouncing upon the ways of God until we either see them finished, or understand their import by a revelation from himself.

VII. Let us be very careful to guard both against presumption and despair; against presumption, in venturing to make our calculations on things not revealed; against despair, into which we may be led by supposing that we already see the end from the beginning. The darkest hour is just before day.

VIII. Meditation on God's providence "should prevent our taking offence, or being discontented at any events rising up before us; for to be displeased at that, which a superior wisdom, unsearchable to us, does order—is to be displeased at we know not what, or why—which is childish weakness. To fret and wail at that which, for all we can see, proceeded from good intention, and tends to a good outcome, is pitiful frowardness."

IX. Let us embrace that mystery of mysteries—the Cross of Christ. He that will reject all mysteries must reject salvation. Let us not cavil—but believe. Wisely did Sir Humphrey Davy say, "If I would choose what would be most delightful, and I believe most useful to me—I would prefer a firm Christian belief to every other blessing." And the great Teacher, who shall also be our final judge, said, "Whoever shall not receive the kingdom of God as a little child shall never enter therein." Will you humbly believe the Gospel? Will you renounce your self-will, your self-sufficiency and your self-righteousness? Well does Mr. Locke say, "Pride of opinion, and arrogance of spirit, are entirely opposed to the humility of true science." Surely then they are opposed to true religion, which has for its basis the sublimest of all knowledge. Will you bow down your haughty spirit and be saved from wrath—by the blood and righteousness of the humblest, meekest and most mysterious sufferer the world ever saw? Oh that you would now be wise! You have but one lifetime, and that will soon be gone. Time flies—Heaven invites—Jesus calls—the Spirit strives—conscience warns—angels wait for your conversion—devils seek your ruin—hell threatens—death approaches—eternity is at the door—the judgment is coming. O humble yourself and believe the Gospel. Believe it *Now*, Now, NOW.

"A point of time, a moment's space,

Removes you to yon heavenly place,
Or shuts you up in hell."

He who rejects the mystery of providence must ever be in perplexity. But he, who rejects the mystery of the cross—must lie down in eternal sorrow.

THE SPECIAL KINDNESS OF PROVIDENCE TOWARDS GODLY MEN

God is unrighteous to none. Yes, he is good to all men—but he shows distinguishing kindness to his people. His sun shines upon both the just and upon the unjust; and he sends rain and fruitful seasons on both the godly and the unthankful. Yet the secret of the Lord is with those who fear him. He governs the incorrigibly wicked, though not in covenant love. Their preservations are reservations for damnation. 2 Pet. 2:9-17. But the life of the righteous is by the Lord mercifully controlled. It is ordered in a manner as kind as it is wise. It is so directed that he and all men shall at last see and say that God is glorified and the eternal good of the believer promoted. We should expect no less. Surely God will not treat friends and foes alike. He never confounds moral distinctions. He is the preserver of all men, "especially of those who believe." "The Lord loves the righteous . . . but the way of the wicked he turns upside down." Psalm 146:8, 9. "All the paths of the Lord are mercy and truth unto such as keep his covenant and his testimonies." Psalm 25:10.

It does not impair the doctrine of a kind and special providence towards the righteous, that they are often involved in the same troubling events with the wicked. This often occurs, as inspired writers admit. "The same destiny ultimately awaits everyone, whether they are righteous or wicked, good or bad, ceremonially clean or unclean, religious or irreligious. Good people receive the same treatment as sinners, and people who take oaths are treated like people who don't." Eccles. 9:2. A pious wife shares with her wicked husband the poverty and misery which his vices bring on them. An invading army overwhelms saints and sinners, with evils which are common to all. The event is the same; but the design, uses and effects are quite different. The purpose of God in afflicting his real people is to make them more useful, more humble, and in the end more glorious. His design in afflicting incorrigible foes is to punish them for their sins, show his wrath, and make them examples of his fearsome justice, as they have been the thankless receivers of countless mercies. So also prosperity awakens the gratitude and refines the feelings of the pious man—but hardens the heart of his wicked neighbor. Thus the prosperity of fools destroys them.

Nor is it a valid objection to the doctrine of a special kind providence over godly men—that they are often more afflicted than the wicked.

First, though "many are the afflictions of the righteous, yet the Lord delivers him out of them all." They do not perish in their affliction.

Secondly, When godly men are "chastened of the Lord, it is that they may not be condemned with the world."

Thirdly, A wise father gives far higher proof of strong and continued love to his child by correcting him than by indulging him, or giving him over to his own follies. Our Father "scourges every son whom he receives."

Fourthly, All the godly confess that to them, even in this life, nothing is more pleasant than the effects of sanctified afflictions; while it is to be lamented that those who lie soft and warm in a rich estate, seldom care to heat themselves at the altar. "No creature can be a substitute for God—but God can be a substitute for every creature." "When we see the peaceable fruits of righteousness, as they hang from the bough of chastisement—we thank God that he ever planted that bitter root in our garden."

Fifthly, By the sadness of the countenance, the heart is made better. "Those the Lord means to make the most resplendent, he has oftenest his tools upon."

Sixthly, If we suffer with him, we shall also reign with him, and all our sorrows shall be found unto praise, and honor, and glory at the appearing of Jesus Christ. So that nothing is more to the advancement of the solid good of the saints in time and eternity than those things which grieve them most. On the other hand the triumph of the wicked is short, their mirth is vain, and it will soon be followed by damnation—a destruction worse than annihilation. Job 20:5; Ecc. 7:6; Psalm 37:35-37; 2 Thess. 1:9. Even in this world the judgments, which overtake the wicked are very dreadful. Gen. 4:13; 1 Sam. 31:4; 2 Chron. 26:19, 20; Acts 1:18; 12:23.

But **we should be very careful not to misinterpret the leadings of Providence**. No doubt Lot thought that God's providence pointed him to Sodom; but he was sadly mistaken. It was the well watered land of the plain that misled him. David knew that God's putting Saul into his power was no opening for murder.

It should be stated, however, that it is not the mere event—but the act of Providence explained by the word of God, which is so beneficial to Christians. Scripture and Providence, like the cherubim over the mercy seat, look toward each other and reflect light upon each other. "The word without Providence is sublime writing," but it is a dead letter; with Providence it is life and spirit.

Providence without the word is a dark enigma. None can solve it. The best commentary on Providence is the Bible. The best commentary on the Bible is Providence. The events of a godly man's life are to him the fulfillings of the Scriptures. In a thousand ways they teach him the true sense of promises and threatenings, predictions and narratives, precepts and doctrines. They mightily confirm his belief of the truth.

And let us not forget that **neither the word of God, nor the Providence of God, without the influences of divine grace on the heart—have a sanctifying power over even godly men. The most striking events and the most precious doctrines will not profit without the promised aid of the Holy Spirit. He can bless any truth or any event to our growth in grace, our comfort and our eternal glory. He is the sanctifier.**

Of course, all the benefit derived from the dealings of God with his people is gracious. Whatever a Christian is, he is by the grace of God, not by nature. No man deplores his own short-comings more than he. He abhors himself; he glories in the Cross of Christ; he is clothed with humility; he is full of kindness; he seeks a heavenly country; his affections are set on things above.

To such a man the providence of God is special and kind. Who can doubt it? The Bible often declares it. "My help comes from the Lord, who made the heavens and the earth! He will not let you stumble and fall; the one who watches over you will not sleep. Indeed, he who watches over Israel never tires and never sleeps. The Lord himself watches over you! The Lord stands beside you as your protective shade. The sun will not hurt you by day, nor the moon at night. The Lord keeps you from all evil and preserves your life. The Lord keeps watch over you as you come and go, both now and forever." Psalm 121:2-8. "He will keep the feet of his saints." 1 Sam. 2:9.

Accordingly inspired men have taught us to pray, "Hold up my goings in your paths, that my footsteps slip not." Psalm 17:5. "Order my steps in your word; and let not any iniquity have dominion over me." Psalm 119:133. The Scripture fully warrants the pious in bringing all their troubles and sorrows before the Lord. They ask and obtain divine guidance and divine support in whatever concerns them. Thus they universally believe with the saints of all ages. Very joyfully therefore do they cast their care upon the Lord, knowing that he cares for them.

Some things in God's providence towards his people are truly surprising. None but the willfully blind can fail to see them. None but the desperately hardened can fail to be affected by them. Let us notice a few of them.

I. The interpositions of Providence for his people are very *seasonable.* They come at the very nick of time. Just as Abram is about to make his son a sacrifice—behold a ram caught in the thicket! Just as Hagar lays down her son to die—God leads her to discover a well of water to save his life! Just as Saul is ready to seize David, and there seems to be no escape to the hunted partridge—that guilty persecutor is called home by an invasion of the Philistines. The very night fixed by a felon to murder a pious widow in a retired neighborhood, and rob her house—God sends a stranger to lodge there and protect her. The very day of his trial for felony, God brings a stranger from a distance to prove the perfect innocence of William Tennent.

Many times in the life of every child of God does he receive the very mercy he needs at a time, when longer delay would be fatal to him. Perhaps for days or weeks he would have fainted unless he had believed that he should see the goodness of God. At last the crisis comes, and his faith must now fail or triumph. To sense all is dark. To mere natural reason nothing is clear. Yet he has hope toward God. Nor is he disappointed. Enlargement and deliverance came just in time to show that none ever trusted in God and was disappointed.

A seasonable mercy is a double mercy. The man in health and without weariness passes by the cooling fountain and cares not for it; but the poor wounded soldier would give anything for one draught of the refreshing beverage which nature has provided. It is a time of persecution. Malice and rage possess the wicked. A city is besieged. The food is exhausted. God's people begin to suffer. To go forth is death by the sword. To remain is death by famine. The city is girt by the sea on one side, and by the merciless foe on all other sides. What shall God's people do? If they could hold out a month, succor would come. But in less than thirty days, they will perish of hunger. Just then an unheard of thing occurs. A shoal of fishes come into that harbor, and all are supplied. The persecutors lose their prey and their hopes. The city is safe. To God give all the people praise.

II. God's interpositions in Providence are just such as the Scriptures have led his people to expect. His word pronounces a blessing on dutiful children. A child gives up all the means of present personal advancement, perhaps even of comfort, to serve a parent; yet who, in the end, was thereby a loser, even in this world? On the other hand, who can find one, who has failed to show piety at home, and whose life has not been rendered unhappy, possibly despicable by such conduct? Again, never did even a wicked man show kindness to a saint of God—but he had his reward. Not only the prophecies—but all the principles of Scripture are wonderfully carried out by the events occurring around us every day, especially in relation to godly men.

III. There is an intimate connection between the providence of God and the prayers of godly men. Where is the experienced saint who has not had answers to prayer so striking and so merciful as greatly to confirm his faith in the promises? And no marvel. For "the eyes of the Lord run to and fro through the whole earth, to show himself strong in behalf of those whose heart is perfect towards him." When lived there a child of God on the earth, who did not have occasion to record what David wrote of himself? "This poor man cried, and the Lord heard him and saved him out of all his troubles." The time would fail to tell of Jacob, and Moses, and Joshua, and Samson, and Jeremiah, and scores of others, whose prayers secured wonderful acts of providence in their behalf. Nor are prayer and providences separated now. Whichever way the humble cries of godly men travel, there travel also the providences of God. "Let Israel hope in the Lord forever and ever."

Alexander Pedan, a Scotch Covenanter, with some others, had been at one time pursued, both by horse and foot, for a considerable way. At last, getting some little distance between them and their pursuers, he stood still and said, "Let us pray here, for if the Lord hear not our prayer and save us, we are all dead men."

He then prayed, saying, "O Lord, this is the hour and the power of your enemies; they may not be idle. But have you no other work for them than to send them after us? Send them after them to whom you will give strength to flee, for our strength is gone. Twine them about the hill, O Lord, save us this one time, and we will keep it in remembrance, and tell to the commendation of your goodness, your pity and compassion, what you did for us at such a time."

And in this he was heard, for a cloud of mist immediately intervened between them and their persecutors; and in the meantime orders came to go in quest of another. See 2 Chron. 18:31.

IV. Nor is God slack in saving his people even if in doing it, many wicked perish. What terrible monuments of his displeasure against his people's enemies did he make of Cain, and Pharaoh, and Haman, and Herod, yes, of Babylon, and Sodom and Gomorrah, and the old world! Nor has he ceased to do like things now. Show me a man of this century, who has spent his breath in curses on God's people, and I will show you one whose history even in this world has commonly marked him out as one forsaken, terribly forsaken of God! It is still true that "he shall have judgment without mercy, who has showed no mercy." It is still true that "bloody and deceitful men shall not live out half their days." When their malice is turned against the righteous, their history is brief; their triumph short, and their doom terrible. **As this world is not the scene of full retribution, all we may expect here is not ample justice—but mere tokens of what God can and will do, when his hand lays hold on vengeance.** Compare 2 Chron. 18:31-34.

V. In some cases we are able to trace a long series of causes and events all conspiring to the same result. The wise men of the East are led to bring from a great distance the most costly presents—articles easily transported—and lay them at the feet of the infant Savior—so that he and Joseph and Mary in their flight to Egypt might have the means of subsistence. Even sometimes to the vision of mortals, perhaps always in the sight of God, **providences are long chains with many links in them. If one link were lacking, the event would fail. But it is God's chain and God's plan. The thing is fixed. The outcome is not doubtful.**

VI. So perfect is God's defense of his people that when appearances all look as if their destruction was imminent, they are still safe. They have fears within and fightings without. They have the world, the flesh and the devil leagued against them. Perhaps there is not a government on earth which has not some anti-Christian legislation, that might become a trap and a snare to a godly man's conscience. The thousandth part of all the wars waged, or the conspiracies formed, and of the blood and treasure expended against Christ's cause—would have rooted out from the earth any institution ever established among men, other than the kingdom of Christ. Still it lives, yes, it flourishes. How is this? The sole answer is, That in Providence, God fulfills his promises, "No weapon formed against you shall prosper," Isaiah 54:17; and, "Though I make a full end of all nations, yet will I not make a full end of you—but I will correct you in measure." Jer. 30:11.

Beziers is besieged. The Protestant cause depends on its safety. The besieged are secure. The bell begins to ring at midnight. Every man is at his post just in time to repel the assault with dismay to the foe. Who rang that alarm bell? Not some faithful sentinel—but a drunken man in a frolic, not knowing what he was doing. Surely God's hand was strikingly in this matter.

Paris is drenched in the gore of Christians. For three days and nights the blood-hounds of regal and papal persecution devour the flock of Christ. His people, who are slain, are gathered home to the Redeemer's bosom. But some of them God would still keep alive for important purposes. One man takes refuge in an oven. His pursuers search diligently for him. They are within a yard of him—but they find him not. Why do they not look into the oven? Just as he entered it, God sent a spider quickly to weave a thick web over its mouth; he then sent a flow of wind to fill the web with dust; and so the bloody men said—Our victim is not here. Thus God saved the life of Du Moulin. Must he not have been an atheist if he could have denied God's hand in this affair? Here is the finger of God.

A thief, who had a few moments before stolen a bottle of warm milk hears a noise, and leaves his bottle in the forest. By this means a persecuted minister and his wife, as they sit sadly down on a rock and find it, are able to give food to their little child, ready to die for lack of nourishment. Marvelous are your works, Lord God Almighty.

VII. God often saves his people by leading them to go where they never intended to go, and where they are sorry to find they have gone, and to do what they never desired to do. The life of Augustine in the 5th century, the life of Dr. John Rodgers of the 18th century, and the life of Rev. William Calhoun of the 19th century were all preserved from destruction from deadly enemies, who hated their doctrine, and lay in wait to put them to death on roads, which these servants of God intended to travel—but from which they unaccountably wandered. "Living and dying do not go by probabilities."

God has one end—man another. Joseph had no design of becoming prime minister of Egypt, temporal savior of the world, and so a type of the great Redeemer, when he told his dreams to his brethren, or when he went to Shechem. Yet had he failed to do either, he had not stood in his lot and fulfilled his course. God's ways are unsearchable and his judgments past finding out.

VIII. Because God is omnipotent and controls all causes, he can rescue as well without miracle, as with it. For three successive days does a copious shower put out the fire kindled by savages to burn alive a prisoner who was a child of prayer. Yet the clouds which dropped down these rains may have arisen entirely under the influence of natural causes. Indeed preservation and other blessings secured to God's people in his ordinary providence are no less safe and certain, and no less fit to be matters of grateful meditation, than if secured by suspending the laws of nature. To a considerate mind they are perhaps even more so. By an act of his will, God could create and send down to each man's door the baked loaves from heaven. Instead of that he waters the earth so that it can be plowed and broken to pieces. He then directs men to sow the wheat, and he sends dew and showers to make it sprout and grow. He then alternately sends the frost and the sun. Perhaps he covers it with a thick, moist mantle of snow. In the spring he sends the melting sun, and plentiful showers. He keeps away harmful insects, and destructive vegetable diseases, and brings the grain to maturity. It is cut; it is dried by the heat he sends; it soon appears in baked loaves on the table. The devout farmer sees God's hand in all the process.

When Merlin, the Chaplain of Admiral Coligny, found his distinguished patron murdered on the melancholy St. Bartholomew's day, he concealed himself in a hay-loft. In the Acts of the next Synod, over which he presided, it is recorded that though many died of hunger, he was supported by a hen regularly laying an egg near his place of refuge. A similar record is made of another French minister, M. de Luce, and a Swabian minister, John Breng, both of whom were kept alive in the same way. To a thoughtful mind ordinary providence is more marvelous than a miracle. The latter is but one act of God, while the former is a series of divine acts working slowly but most surely.

A noble is suspected of treason. He is arrested and imprisoned. In the yard to his dungeon between the paving stones springs up a little flower. He watches it. He waters it. He cares for it. It grows. He writes the history of its development and growth. This narrative is God's appointed means of effecting his release. See a little book called 'Picciola'.

IX. God's providence towards his people dates not at the time of their being called to a knowledge of himself—but long before. In the formation of their bodies, what goodness appears. No man has ever been able to suggest how the form or figure of the human frame could be improved. In this indeed the wicked share the same bounty of God. In their early infancy how amazing was God's care over them. Think too of the early and deep impressions which God often makes on the minds and hearts of his chosen, even years before their conversion. In a solitary forest among huge rocks, or hoary mountains, or by some gentle stream, or noble river, or vast expanse of waters, what conceptions of God has many a child had! In an escape from danger—what a sense of God's goodness has stolen over the hearts of his people, even before their conversion. John Brown of Haddington tells us of his deep pious impressions at a sacramental meeting, when he was under ten years of age. The late Archibald Alexander, when only four years and a half old, was greatly interested in a sermon on 1 Cor. 16:22. Even where such impressions do not end in a speedy conversion, they are often very beneficial in preserving the young from the worst forms of evil.

Nor is anything more wonderful than **the means God uses for the conversion of his people**. A sermon, in which the preacher had no knowledge and no design respecting the spiritual good of any particular person—a sermon by a weak man addressed to those who had often heard much better discourses on the same topics—a text of Scripture learned twenty years before—a little portion of truth found on a piece of wrapping-paper—a sudden death of some wicked man—the death of some godly man—a pious book—a kind word—a look of tenderness—the consistent piety of a pious wife, husband or friend—and even the profaneness of wicked men—have been the means of bringing sinners to repentance.

Many a man has been led to the Savior by truths, which the preacher did not intend to utter when he began his discourse. Augustine tells us of a celebrated Manachee who was thus converted under the labors of the bishop of Hippo. Paul and Silas were not the only prisoners who were honored by God as the means of converting their hardened jailors. Had the persecution not arisen at Jerusalem, Philip would not have fallen in with the Ethiopian returning to his own country and reading Isaiah. So that great man might have died in ignorance of the true meaning of the prophet. Many a man has gone for no good end to hear a sermon, and before the discourse was ended has forgotten what he came for and has begun to cry for mercy.

X. God's providence in raising up good ministers of various gifts to edify his church is truly striking. It is the time of the American Revolution. A company is drilling and firing by platoons.

In the ranks is a malicious man, who wishes to have his spite on a particular family. He loads that man's gun so heavily, that he knows firing it off will burst the barrel of his gun. Just before firing, he unsuspectingly calls a lad in the crowd to take his place. The impulsive boy, suspecting no harm, consents, fires the gun, and his left hand is shattered. Amputation is necessary. This cruel act gives a new direction to his whole life. His parents send him to a classical school taught by a pious man. The youth learns well, in due time becomes a Christian, is finally ordained to the Gospel ministry, bears the name of the preacher with the silver fist and the silver voice, with great power addresses thousands in the open air, and dies greatly lamented leaving a noble posterity behind him. Such was the history of Drury Lacy.

Some boys are pursuing a rabbit. It takes refuge in a hollow log. While one boy is attempting to cut it out, another puts in his arm, trying to reach his prey. The axe cripples his hand for life. He is educated, becomes a herald of salvation and leaves a precious memory in all the land. When Patrick Henry heard him discourse on the creation, he said it seemed to him as if that man could almost make a world. His name was James Waddell.

Many a time by the feebleness of their bodies, parental plans respecting the temporal conduct of their children are defeated, and parental pity at last consents to their commencing studies which may give them the learning so useful to preachers of the Gospel. In due time God calls them to a knowledge of himself and of his Son. Then by his Spirit he calls them to preach the unsearchable riches of Christ. To others, whom God designs for great hardships in the ministry, he gives great vigor of constitution, so that they can bear almost any amount of labor and weariness. How marvelous also is God's providence in the mental and social character naturally possessed by his people, so as to fit them to act their several parts in life. In illustration look at the ministers of Christ. One is timid, and God makes him especially useful to the diffident in encouraging them, and to the self-confident in awakening beneficial fears. Another is bold, and he alarms the guilty and encourages the wavering. One is full of love and so wins the skeptic and melts the hardened. Another is borne down by an awful sense of the danger of the wicked, and so he cries aloud and spares not. One is a son of thunder. Another is a son of consolation. One excels in logic, another in rhetoric. One is best at explaining the doctrines, another is excellent at exhortation. One does most good by his pen, another by private conversation, and another in the pulpit. Yet all these men are giving expression to their respective natural and social dispositions, now sanctified by divine grace, and turned to a holy work. Like acts of providence may be noticed in the variety of character displayed by all his people.

XI. When means have been blessed to the conversion of his people, how strange the providences of God which lead to their growth in grace! They are ready to lean on one minister; and God takes him away and sends another. They think affliction would do them good, and God makes his mercies overflow. Or they think prosperity best for them, and God crosses all their plans and spoils their pleasant things. They are self-confident and fear not falling into sin, and soon a sad lapse fills their hearts with anguish. They are much afraid of bringing dishonor on their profession, and their fears are blessed to their preservation from sin. John Newton, who has often edified the church of God, has well described this matter, when he says—

"I asked the Lord, that I might grow
In faith, and love and every grace;
Might more of his salvation know,
And seek more earnestly his face.

"Twas He who taught me thus to pray,
And He, I trust has answered prayer;
But it has been in such a way
As almost drove me to despair.

"I hoped that in some favored hour,
At once he'd answer my request;
And by His love's constraining power,
Subdue my sins and give me rest.

"Instead of this He made me feel
The hidden evils of my heart,
And let the angry powers of hell
Assault my soul in every part.

"Yes, more; with His own hand He seemed
Intent to aggravate my woe;
Crossed all the fair designs I schemed,
Blasted my gourds, and laid me low.

"'Lord, why is this?' I trembling cried,
'Will you pursue your worm to death?'
'This is this way,' the Lord replied,
'I answer prayer for grace and faith.'

"'These inward trials I employ
From self and pride to set you free,
And break your schemes of earthly joy,
That you would seek your all in me."

XII. Go among God's people and learn how goodly in many ways their lot has been. What pious **parents** most of them have had. How wonderfully God has led them in many important steps in life. How pleasant have been their friends and their children. Even the little ones, whom Jesus has early called to himself, seem still to warm and nestle in the bosom of parental love. How many good **books** they have had to read. What kind and skillful physicians have attended them in sickness. When disease has come upon them, what good places they have had to be sick in. How infrequent and short their bodily infirmities commonly are. How seldom have they suffered for the lack of suitable food, or clothing, or shelter, or any necessary thing. How marked the hand of God in ordering the general tenor of their lives. Often have their feet well near slipped—but God has held them up. They have been in the midst of almost all evil—but it has not been allowed to sweep them away. How often has God "hedged up their way with thorns, and made a wall that they could not find their paths." Hos. 2:6. Often they could not perform their enterprises—which would have proved their ruin. Job 5:12. The unseen dangers from men and devils, from friends and foes, from darkness and pestilence surrounding us—are far more numerous than those which are visible. Could we have seen them all as God saw them, our lives would probably have been full of misery. How kind his providence in giving us a heart and temper to enjoy life and its mercies.

XIII. Toward his people, God's providence is exceedingly rich in spiritual blessings. It embraces a plan reaching from eternity to eternity. It is set forth in a covenant ordered in all things and sure, an everlasting covenant, having the Lord Jesus Christ for a Surety and Mediator. God's loving-kindness laid the foundation of the whole scheme of redemption. It shall lay the top-stone in glory. It orders everything aright forever. Thus far the history of redemption has no parallel. It is God's chief work—the wonder of angels—the joy of saints. The whole subject seems to abash the faculties of all right-minded creatures. **The sea of Jehovah's compassion and wisdom has never been fathomed by men or angels.** Under the conduct of providence it will be widening its shores and deepening its abysses forever.

Practical Remarks on the Special Kindness of Providence Towards Godly Men

I. What a theme for humble, devout and joyous meditation have we in this doctrine of providence! The pious Flavel says, "It will doubtless be a part of our entertainment in *heaven* to view with transporting delight, how the designs and methods were laid to bring us there—and what will be a part of our blessedness in *heaven* may be well allowed to have a prime ingredient into our heaven upon earth. To search for pleasure among the due observations of Providence is to search for water in the ocean." In a like strain the amiable John Howe says, "When the records of eternity shall be exposed to view, all the counsels and results of the profound wisdom looked into—how will it transport, when it shall be discovered! Lo, thus were the designs laid; here were the apt junctures and admirable dependencies of things, which, when acted upon the stage of time, seemed so perplexed and intricate."

Let God's "loving-kindness" be continually before your eyes. Think on his judgments. "He who will observe the wonderful providences of God—shall have wonderful providences of God to observe." "Whoever is wise, and will observe these things, even they shall understand the loving-kindness of the Lord." Charnock says, "It is a part of atheism to think the acts of God in the world are not worth our serious thoughts. God is highly angry with those that mind him not. 'Because they regard not the operation of his hands, he shall destroy them, and not build them up.'" Psalm 28:5. It is a divine art, to view the hand of God in everything. It is an ennobling employment to meditate on all the wonders he has wrought. "The works of the Lord are great, sought out by all those who have pleasure therein." Psalm 111:2. That was a good resolution of Asaph, "I will remember the works of the Lord; surely I will remember your wonders of old—I will meditate also of all your work, and talk of your doings." Psalm 77:11, 12.

II. There is excellent wisdom in our Savior's saying, "What I do you know not now—but hereafter you shall know it." In this world nothing in providence is fully finished. Judge artists or artisans by appearances when their work is but half done—and not one of them could stand so unfair a test. Peter was greatly opposed to Christ's dying at all. The disciples were overwhelmed when he did die. But out of his death sprang the life of the world. There would have been no gospel to believe or to preach, had Jesus not died. God's "way is in the sea, and his path in the great waters, and his footsteps are not known." Psalm 77:19. A carpenter's rule is too short to measure the heavens with. The waters of the sea can never be contained in a bottle. Neither can *we* ever fully know any act of providence as God knows it. But to judge of an event before the final issue is great folly. It is also sin. It is both arrogant and presumptuous. It also brings much misery with it.

Who is more wretched than the man, who sees nothing but desolating storms in every cloud, nothing but disaster in every undertaking, nothing but sorrow in the very means used for his joy, nothing but overthrow in the steps which lead to his exaltation? Oh for a stronger faith. Oh for more patience. Could we but calmly wait and let the God of all the earth do as he pleases, all would be well. **We are so wrapped up in selfishness that we flagrantly over-estimate the importance of our own affairs.**

A splendid steamer is swiftly passing up the Mississippi. She has more than five hundred passengers, pressing home to soothe sorrow, or scatter joy, to give life to commerce, and to carry messages of government. Vast interests depend on her safety and her speed. A little boy darts into the cafeteria, crying for the captain. At length he finds him, and says, "O captain, stop the boat, do stop the boat!" "Why, my son?" said the veteran officer. The boy replied, "I have dropped my orange overboard, do stop the boat." He was told it could not be done. His solicitude settled into sadness, which left him only after sleep. Think of that boy and his orange. There was some proportion between the value of that orange—and the other interests involved, yet it was exceedingly small. But there is no proportion between our comfort for a day—and the glory of God to eternity; or between our afflictions here—and the glory that shall be revealed in us hereafter. "Be patient, brethren, unto the coming of our Lord Jesus Christ." **We know not what is best for us.** Foolish children eat green apples—but prudent people first let them mature. Let us trust God joyfully. Psalm 27:6.

III. How entirely do just views of God's word and providence

change the aspects of everything. He, who has any right views, would rather be with Shadrach, Meshach and Abednego in the furnace, or with Daniel in the lions' den—than with Nebuchadnezzar on the throne. Paul bound with a chain was far more to be envied than Nero wearing the imperial purple. Paul and Silas were far from being the most unhappy men in Philippi the night their feet were in the stocks. There are two sides to every providence, as there were to the pillar of cloud and of fire. The bright side is towards the children of God. It ever will be so. God has ordained it. He will make good all his promises. "Light is sown for the righteous, and gladness for the upright." Therefore, you heroes of the cross of Christ—gird on your armor. Fight the good fight of faith. Never yield to fear. Endure hardness. Live to please him who has called you to be soldiers. Jesus reigns! Hear him proclaiming, "All power in heaven and earth is given unto me." He is King of kings. He rules in the kingdoms of men. He is God in Zion. He loves the church more than you do. He died for it. He loves his people as the apple of his eye. Nothing shall harm those who are the followers of his cross. O shout and give thanks. Robert Southwell, awaiting martyrdom in prison, wrote to his friend, "We have sung the canticles of the Lord in a strange land, and in this desert we have sucked honey from the rock, and oil from the hard flint." Learn this heavenly art!

IV. Sinners, will not you give your hearts to God, and secure the blessings of his kindness, the care of his special providence? Do you not need a Father in heaven? Do you not wish for a shield and buckler and horn of salvation? Persisting in sin and folly—the stars will fight against you in their courses. Yielding to the claims of divine love and authority—all nature will at Jehovah's bidding fight for you. Will you bow your neck? Will you take Christ's yoke upon you? Will you be saved?

V. The *right* observance of providence is a great duty. The particulars of this duty are well stated by Thomas Boston—

1. We should watch for them until they come. Heb. 2:1-3; Psalm 130:1, 5, 6; Lam. 3:49, 50.
2. We should take heed to them, and mark them when they come. Isaiah 25:9; Ezek. 1:15; Zech. 6: Luke 19:44.
3. We should seriously review them, ponder and closely consider them. Psalm 111:2; Ezek. 10:13; Psalm 73:16; Job 10:2; Psalm 77:6.
4. We should lay them up, and keep them in record. Luke 1:66; 1 Sam. 17:37; Psalm 37:25.
5. We should observe them for practical purposes, that they may

have a sanctifying power over our hearts and lives. Psalm 64:7, 9; Deut. 29:2, 3, 4; 2 Kings 6:33; Ecc. 7:14.

ALTERNATE LIGHT AND DARKNESS IN PROVIDENCE, ILLUSTRATED IN THE CASE OF THE GREAT MAN OF UZ

The book of Job is the oldest and the best epic poem in the world. The people prominently before us are Jehovah, Satan, Job, Job's wife, his three friends, Eliphaz, Bildad and Zophar, and that remarkable person, Elihu. Much of the book is a discussion of the principles, on which the speakers suppose God's providence to be conducted.

Some have surmised that Job was a fictitious character; but this is surely a mistake. The prophet Ezekiel clearly proves that he was a historic personage—as much so as Noah or Daniel. Ezek. 14:14, 20. He was a man, and a very godly man.

The course of providence towards him is full of instruction. In his life we find lessons of much value. Instruction by *example* clearly points out the duty to be performed, shows that it is practical, and awakens in the virtuous the desire of imitation.

Among mere men we seldom find a striking example of more than one striking feature. Abraham was distinguished for his faith; Moses, for his meekness; Daniel, for his dauntlessness; John, for the tenderness of his love; and Job, for his patience. If we would find perfect symmetry of character in any portion of history, we must go to the man Christ Jesus.

It may aid us to pursue a method in our reflections.

I. Let us consider the course of providence towards Job, and his character and circumstances before his great afflictions. Job was a man of great piety. The Scriptures say that he was upright and perfect. He was not double-tongued, nor double-minded—but sincere, free from hypocrisy, and had respect to all God's commandments. "He feared God and eschewed evil." This character is given by God himself. His reputation among men was both fair and high. "Those were the days when I went to the city gate and took my place among the honored leaders. The young stepped aside when they saw me, and even the aged rose in respect at my coming. The princes stood in silence and put their hands over their mouths. The highest officials of the city stood quietly, holding their tongues in respect. All who heard of me praised me. All who saw me spoke well of me." Job 29:8-10. Probably no man ever received more marked attention from great and small than did Job. "Everyone listened to me and valued my advice. They were silent as they waited for me to speak. And after I spoke, they had nothing to add, for my counsel satisfied them. They longed for me to speak as they longed for rain. They waited eagerly, for my words were as refreshing as the spring rain. When they were discouraged, I smiled at them. My look of approval was precious to them." Job 29:21-24

He was also esteemed wise, and possessed great influence by his eloquence. He was a sound adviser. Speaking of his influence over men, it is said, "I told them what they should do and presided over them as their chief." Job 29:25.

Job was also a great captain. His military skill and prowess were such that he dwelt as king in the army. Job 29:25. "He broke the jaws of the wicked, and plucked the spoil out of his teeth." Job 29:17. He was also a philanthropist. He was not indeed ostentatious in his charity, yet such a city set on a hill cannot be hid. "All who heard of me praised me. All who saw me spoke well of me. For I helped the poor in their need and the orphans who had no one to help them. I helped those who had lost hope, and they blessed me. And I caused the widows' hearts to sing for joy. All I did was just and honest. Righteousness covered me like a robe, and I wore justice like a turban. I served as eyes for the blind and feet for the lame. I was a father to the poor and made sure that even strangers received a fair trial." Job 29:11-16. In his labors of love, he was both diligent and unselfish.

Before his afflictions Job was a man of great wealth. "He owned seven thousand sheep, three thousand camels, five hundred teams of oxen, and five hundred female donkeys, and he employed many servants. He was, in fact, the richest person in that entire area." Job 1:3. In wealth he excelled all the rich men of the East. So abundant were his possessions that "my path was drenched with cream and the rock poured out for me streams of olive oil."

In his own family, Job enjoyed domestic comfort. Although he had his fears about his children, yet it does not appear that they were either profane or licentious. He loved them tenderly and they were respectful to him. His wife seems not to have shown her grievous lack of piety during his prosperity.

To crown all his enjoyments, the candle of the Lord shined upon his head, and by the light of the divine countenance he walked through darkness. The secret of God was upon his tabernacle, and the Almighty was yet with him. Job 29:3-5. It is in God's light that we see light. When he smiles we are blessed. When he gives comfort, who can afflict? All this prosperity begat confidence in its own continuance, and led Job to say, "I shall die in my nest and I shall multiply my days as the sand. My root was spread out by the waters, and the dew lay all night upon my branch. My glory was fresh in me, and my bow was renewed in my hand." Job 29:18-20.

II. Let us consider Job's afflictions themselves, and his patience under them.

One day when Job's sons and daughters were dining at the oldest brother's house, a messenger arrived at Job's home with this news: "Your oxen were plowing, with the donkeys feeding beside them, when the Sabeans raided us. They stole all the animals and killed all the farmhands. I am the only one who escaped to tell you." While he was still speaking, another messenger arrived with this news: "The fire of God has fallen from heaven and burned up your sheep and all the shepherds. I am the only one who escaped to tell you." While he was still speaking, a third messenger arrived with this news: "Three bands of Chaldean raiders have stolen your camels and killed your servants. I am the only one who escaped to tell you." While he was still speaking, another messenger arrived with this news: "Your sons and daughters were feasting in their oldest brother's home. Suddenly, a powerful wind swept in from the desert and hit the house on all sides. The house collapsed, and all your children are dead. I am the only one who escaped to tell you!" Job 1:13-19

A descent from such extraordinary prosperity awakens very different sentiments from those entertained by men, who have long lived in poor circumstances and been unexpectedly raised to greatness. Let this thought be remembered.

Job's afflictions commenced with the loss of his wealth, consisting of oxen, and donkeys, and sheep, and camels, and servants. The news of these losses came upon him by surprise. Poverty is no sin—if it comes upon us without any fault of ours. Yet everyone knows that it brings sore trials on all, especially on those who are not accustomed to it. All this is heightened by the suddenness of its approach. This often produces a shock which few hearts are sufficiently stout to resist. Many who have stood calm while thrones were falling around them, who have fearlessly stormed the deadly breach, and who have manfully suffered community slander, have sunk under intolerable anguish, when their earthly possessions have taken flight and left them destitute and dependent. Whatever bitterness is necessarily connected with such loss, was the portion of Job.

No sooner had the messengers closed their respective narratives of his losses of property, than another with all the promptness attending the announcement of calamities thus spoke, "Your sons and daughters were feasting in their oldest brother's home. Suddenly, a powerful wind swept in from the desert and hit the house on all sides. The house collapsed, and all your children are dead. I am the only one who escaped to tell you!" Thus his children were carried into eternity on the same day on which he lost all his property! Not a child was left him. His Reuben and his Benjamin, his daughter that was to him as a pet lamb, and she that was in deportment as a matron, all died. And then they died so suddenly. No previous sickness gave warning of approaching death. In the morning he had parted with them, not dreaming that he would nevermore see their faces in the land of the living. Nor had he satisfactory evidence that they were prepared for this solemn exchange of worlds. Indeed he had fears to the contrary. As priest of his own house, he had been in the habit of offering sacrifices for them on occasion of their feasts, thinking that they might have sinned and cursed God in their hearts. Job 1:5. But on this occasion Job had not time to offer sacrifice or prayer after the close of the feast. How must this saint of God have followed in imagination the departed spirits of his children. And how must his heart have swollen with anguish when in vain he sought for assurance of their salvation. Yet at the end of all this, Job reverently "fell down upon the ground, and worshiped, and said, Naked came I out of my mother's womb and naked shall I return there—the Lord gave, and the Lord has taken away; blessed be the name of the Lord." Job 1:20, 21.

But neither the malignity of Satan, nor the mysterious love of God, would permit Job's sufferings to end here. Satan obtained permission to afflict him with bodily disease, so that he was covered from the sole of his foot unto his crown with sore boils. This affliction makes a standing posture a rack of torture, a chair a seat of misery, and a couch a "bed of unrest." In the midst of his wretchedness, he "took a potsherd to scrape himself and he sat down in the ashes." In our suffering it is seldom that we cannot find some posture that will not give some relief. But this was not Job's case. Pain followed pain, and suffering followed suffering—until his agony was complete. Hear his dolorous complaint, "I, too, have been assigned months of futility, long and weary nights of misery. When I go to bed, I think, 'When will it be morning?' But the night drags on, and I toss till dawn. My skin is filled with worms and scabs. My flesh breaks open, full of pus." Job 7:3-5

From all this weight of suffering Job might have found some relief, had his wife possessed a right spirit. But when she saw him thus afflicted, her heart rose in rebellion against God, and instead of exhorting her husband to faith and patience, she bade him "curse God and die." During his prosperity Job's wife may have given some evidence of piety. If so, how must such an avowal have pierced his soul; and if not, how afflicting it must have been to behold her, whom he loved so tenderly, venting her wickedness against God? She not only manifested hatred to him whom Job adored; but she became cold and cruel to her husband. He says, "My breath is repulsive to my wife. I am loathsome to my own family." Job 19:17. The appeal to marital affection was fruitless. Pointing to the pledges of their love in their offspring had no effect. Her marriage vows and all the kindness she had received, were forgotten. Her heart was unfeeling.

Another source of distress to Job was the conduct of his friends, his servants and his neighbors. To him who is afflicted, pity should be shown. But when those in whom we have trusted hide as it were their faces from us, it is sad indeed. At first Job's friends seemed disposed to sympathize with him—but they soon began to accuse him wrongfully. They aggravated his sufferings by referring to his former prosperity. Job 4:2. They dealt deceitfully with him. Job 6:15. They scorned him. Job 16:20. They vexed his soul. Job 19:2. He says, "They whom I loved, have turned against me." Job 19:19. They charged him with hypocrisy, Job 20:5; they told him God was punishing him for his injustice and cruelty, Job 22:6-9; they perverted his language, and upon his speech put a construction which he had never thought of, and a meaning which he abhorred. Job 34:9; 35:2.

The great difficulty was that without evidence they believed him guilty of great sins; and such people cannot be convinced by evidence. Under these circumstances Job poured forth his complaints. Hear him—"My relatives stay far away, and my friends have turned against me. My neighbors and my close friends are all gone. The members of my household have forgotten me. The servant girls consider me a stranger. I am like a foreigner to them. I call my servant, but he doesn't come; I even plead with him!" Job 19:13-16. So full was the conviction of those around Job that he was a wicked man, and so helpless was he, that he was held in the utmost contempt. "Even young children despise me. When I stand to speak, they turn their backs on me. My close friends abhor me. Those I loved have turned against me." Job 19:18-19.

The children of the vilest men, mocked him and spit in his face. "But now I am mocked by those who are younger than I, by young men whose fathers are not worthy to run with my sheepdogs. And now their sons mock me with their vulgar song! They taunt me! They despise me and won't come near me, except to spit in my face." Job 30.

If we feel great pain at even suspicion thrown on our characters, what must Job's anguish have been when old and young, rich and poor, vile and honorable, pious and ungodly united in suspecting, condemning or despising him as a wicked man!

Nor had Job any means of proving himself innocent. The charges brought against him were general and vague. It was impossible for him to prove a negative. Yet he felt, as all godly men do, that a good name is better than great riches and precious ointment. His other trials would have been comparatively light, had his friends been true and kind. But they were unstable and greatly misjudged him.

Another source of sorrow was that Job had no *sensible* pious comfort. He cries out, "Oh that I were as in months past." Job 29:2. At no period of his sufferings does he seem to have had those transporting views of divine things, which many of the martyrs had, and which quenched the violence of fire, and bore the soul away from the consideration of personal pains—to rapturous thoughts on Jesus, and heaven, and the crown of imperishable glory. Yes, not only was he tossed with tempest and not comforted—but his soul was filled with great distress. He cries out, "For the Almighty has struck me down with his arrows. He has sent his poisoned arrows deep within my spirit. All God's terrors are arrayed against me!" Job 6:4. The spirit of a man sustains his infirmity—but a wounded spirit who can bear? Even when alone, the terrors of God may be insupportable; but when joined to so many other evils, where is the heart strong enough to bear the dreadful weight?

It heightened Job's misery that he had not sweet access to God by prayer. He says, "If only I knew where to find God, I would go to his throne and talk with him there. I would lay out my case and present my arguments. Then I would listen to his reply and understand what he says to me. I go east, but he is not there. I go west, but I cannot find him. I do not see him in the north, for he is hidden. I turn to the south, but I cannot find him." Job 23. The privilege of prayer in all its sweetness remaining to God's people, they have inexpressible comfort; but when that is gone, what can the soul do?

Another aggravation of Job's affliction was, that although better instructed than his friends, **he yet but imperfectly understood the doctrine of providence**. This difficulty has been felt in every age. In the patriarchal and Mosaic dispensations it terribly afflicted the righteous. Even under the clear light of the gospel, godly men have perplexities from this source. Job had no such clear Scriptures as these, "As many as I love, I rebuke and chasten." "If you be without chastisement, you are not sons." "We must through much tribulation enter the kingdom of God." "We know that all things work together for good to those who love God." Instead of this clear light Job himself saw God's ways involved in inscrutable mystery. Job 31:3.

Hope of better days on earth seems quite to have departed from him. He says, "I shall no more see good." Job 7:7. As far forward as his vision extended, all was dark and dreary. No star of promise, no ray of joyous expectation illumined the gloom. Former greatness and happiness but showed him how low he had fallen. They gave no pledge of return. All seemed to be irretrievably gone to the great man of Uz. "So I looked for good, but evil came instead. I waited for the light, but darkness fell. My heart is troubled and restless. Days of affliction have come upon me. I walk in gloom, without sunlight. I stand in the public square and cry for help. But instead, I am considered a brother to jackals and a companion to ostriches. My skin has turned dark, and my bones burn with fever. My harp plays sad music, and my flute accompanies those who weep." Job 30:26-31

Under this enormous load of suffering Job set a bright example of patience. Not a word of sinful murmur escaped his lips. Job 1:22. He exhibited not the proud severity of the stoic in refusing to acknowledge himself afflicted. He had not the iron hardihood of atheism, denying God's hand in his troubles. Nor did he exhibit the sinful sinking of unbelief. **He submissively acquiesced in what God ordained.** He brought no foolish charge against his Maker. He meekly says, "What? shall we receive good at the hand of God—and shall we not receive evil?" Job 2:10. He sought solace in worship and especially in praise. It is not claimed that in all things Job was spotlessly pure—but only that he was in the main and persistently upright. Near the close of the book God himself says, "My servant Job has spoken of me that which is right." Job 42:7. Job did indeed undertake to reason on matters beyond his knowledge. Job 38:2. But the general tenor of his feelings was pleasing to God. For a long time he bore the most trying events with a spirit of submission probably never equaled in a mere man. For this cause he is fitly held up to us as one whose example is worthy of imitation.

III. Let us consider Job's history after the heavy hand of God was no longer upon him. On this point the record is brief but highly satisfactory. "When Job prayed for his friends, the Lord restored his fortunes. In fact, the Lord gave him twice as much as before! Then all his brothers, sisters, and former friends came and feasted with him in his home. And they consoled him and comforted him because of all the trials the Lord had brought against him. And each of them brought him a gift of money and a gold ring. So the Lord blessed Job in the second half of his life even more than in the beginning. For now he had fourteen thousand sheep, six thousand camels, one thousand teams of oxen, and one thousand female donkeys. He also gave Job seven more sons and three more daughters. He named his first daughter Jemimah, the second Keziah, and the third Keren-happuch. In all the land there were no other women as lovely as the daughters of Job. And their father put them into his will along with their brothers. Job lived 140 years after that, living to see four generations of his children and grandchildren. Then he died, an old man who had lived a long, good life." Job 42:10-17.

Every foul imputation on his character was wiped away. Every slanderous tongue was silenced. The terrible storm was passed. Only the peaceable fruits of righteousness remained. Sobered and chastened he indeed was—but richly laden with the experience of God's goodness. He saw the end of the Lord, that the Lord is full of pity and of tender mercy.

CONCLUDING OBSERVATIONS

1. How vain are all merely earthly possessions! How unstable is popular favor! How uncertain are riches! How soon our pleasures may be followed by pains! When parents rejoice at the birth of a child, they know not how soon they may weep over his dead body without an assurance that his soul is saved. Solomon thoroughly tried the world. His sober inspired judgment was that all was vanity. The sooner we reach that conclusion ourselves—the wiser shall we be! "Meaningless! Meaningless! Utterly meaningless! Everything is meaningless!" Ecclesiastes 1:2. Now all has been heard; here is the conclusion of the matter: Fear God and keep his commandments, for this is the whole duty of man. For God will bring every deed into judgment, including every hidden thing, whether it is good or evil." Ecclesiastes 12:13-14.

2. Let us always be more afraid of sinning against God than of offending our nearest earthly friends. Job instantly repulsed the wicked assaults of his wife, saying, "You speak as one of the foolish women speaks." Job 2:10. To his own disciple, Peter, Jesus was compelled to say, "Get behind me, Satan! You are a stumbling block to me; you do not have in mind the things of God, but the things of men." Matt. 16:23. No human friendship may for a moment interfere with our fidelity to God.

3. Although God generally chooses the poor as his children, yet he offers mercy to the rich, and receives all such as humbly seek his grace. Job's riches did not debar him from the kingdom of heaven. By reason of depravity, riches tend to alienate the heart from God; yet sovereign grace can remedy that evil. He, who is rich in this world's goods, and also rich in faith and good works, is loudly called to sing the praises of Jehovah. Nothing but almighty power could thus make the camel go through the eye of the needle, or preserve the soul from the burning flames of insatiable covetousness.

4. Weight of character and a high order of talents are by no means confined to the enemies of God. Why should they be? Piety is wisdom. Whoever stood higher for wisdom in council, for soundness of judgment and for prowess in war than did the man of Uz? There cannot be found any number of men who surpass God's

people for calmness of inquiry, soberness of mind and practical wisdom. True religion is worthy of the most earnest and solemn attention.

5. Christian men are not always pious, in proportion to the degree of light which they enjoy. Job is supposed to have lived before the time of Moses, under the obscurity of the patriarchal dispensation; yet he was a burning and a shining light. He neither saw nor heard many wondrous things well known to us. Yet how far did he and Abraham and Enoch and other ancient worthies excel the great mass of even godly men of these latter days. Truly we ought to blush for our short-comings. Guilt is in proportion to light. Surely then we must be very guilty for our sad deficiencies.

6. When malice, or envy, or suspicion, or evil surmising exists—no established reputation, no lack of evidence of guilt can "tie the gall up in the slanderous tongue." By a long and holy life Job had given incontestable evidence of the purity of his character. His friends could bring no proof of his criminality in anything. Yet they charged him with cruelty, wickedness and hypocrisy! Such vileness has not yet left the earth. It is no new or rare thing for the best men to be charged with the vilest plans, principles or practices. It will be so until grace shall reign through Jesus Christ over all hearts. A propensity to evil thoughts and evil speeches, is among the last faults of character, from which even godly men are delivered.

7. If friends accuse us falsely and act as enemies, let us not forget to pray for them. Job set us the example—Job 42:8. Enmities arising between old friends are generally more violent than others. "A brother offended is harder to be won than a strong city—and their contentions are like the bars of a castle." Proverbs 18:19. But we must not yield to evil passion. We must forgive and seek blessings on those who falsely accuse us and cruelly entreat us. It was not until Job prayed for his accusers that God turned his captivity. Let us never carry a load of malice in our hearts. It is worse than any evil we can suffer at the hand of man.

8. When our characters are assailed, we are at liberty to use Christian measures to remove an evil report. It is then best to leave the whole matter in the hands of God. Lawsuits for character may be lawful and sometimes expedient. But when bad passions are excited, no character is so unspotted that malice will not spew out its venom against it. We may deny our guilt; we may call for evidence against us; we may bring evidence of innocence; but with men of heated imaginations and strong prejudices, evidence never

has its just weight.

9. **It is very dangerous to become involved in a labyrinth of reasoning concerning God, his character and providence.** Things which are revealed belong to us and our children. We may safely follow wherever revelation leads; but we are no judges of what is proper to be done under the government of God. The attempt to criticize the divine proceedings is always a failure and iniquity. "The secret things belong to the Lord our God, but the things revealed belong to us and to our children forever, that we may follow all the words of this law." Deuteronomy 29:29. "For my thoughts are not your thoughts, neither are your ways my ways," declares the LORD. "As the heavens are higher than the earth, so are my ways higher than your ways and my thoughts than your thoughts." Isaiah 55:8-9.

10. It is important to study the Scriptures and learn all we can concerning the plans and providence of God. Had Job clearly known what we by patient study may learn, it would have removed much of the pungency of his grief. God's word is a light and a lamp. Let us walk by it.

11. What is the grief of each one? Is it poverty, poor health, loss of reputation, loss of pious comfort? Whatever it is, take for an example of suffering affliction Job—the narrative of whose trials was written for our comfort. Like him, let each one say of the Almighty, "Though he slays me, yet will I trust in him." Job 13:15. Never was pious confidence in the Lord misplaced. Never did any trust in him and was confounded.

12. The secret of the Lord is with those who fear him. The greatest secret God ever reveals to his people is the mystery of redemption. Of this Job was not ignorant. By this he triumphed. His own language is explicit, "But as for me—I know that my Redeemer lives, and that he will stand upon the earth at last. And after my body has decayed, yet in my body I will see God! I will see him for myself! Yes, I will see him with my own eyes! I am overwhelmed at the thought!" Job 19:25-27.

GOD'S PROVIDENCE TOWARDS HIS CHURCH RENDERS UNNECESSARY

ALL TORMENTING FEARS RESPECTING HER SAFETY AND FINAL TRIUMPH

The fear of the Lord is the beginning of wisdom—of this kind of fear, we cannot have too much. There is also a beneficial fear, based in self-distrust, and opposed to pride and carelessness. That is a good quality. Blessed is the man who thus always fears.

But there is also a fear which torments. It disheartens, multiplies difficulties, magnifies obstacles, and refuses available resources. Such fear brings a snare. It begets doubts and despondency. It cries—There is a lion in the way. It weeps when it should rejoice. It sings dirges when paeans of praise are called for. It is in many ways an enemy to our peace and usefulness. It is a grief to our fellows. It is an offence to God.

Sometimes such fear possesses the church. She trembles for her own safety. Let us consider the matter in order.

I. THE OCCASIONS OF THIS FEAR are such as these—

1. When the church looks to herself for resources and encouragement. She is "a little flock." "Jacob is small." The people of God are "a remnant." The house of God cannot boast of great numbers. Much as Zion has lengthened her cords beyond her former possessions, she is still but a garden hedged in. Few love her feasts, or delight in her solemnities. Her outward state is humble. Most of her friends are poor. In gathering his family, the Lord refuses none who sincerely apply for admission; yet generally he pours contempt on princes, stains the pride of all glory, takes the beggar from the ash-heap and exalts him to sonship with God. Zion's friends are an afflicted people. "She is black as the tents of Kedar. The sun has looked upon her." Waters of a full cup are wrung out to her children. Her garments are stained in the blood of her martyrs. She is very feeble. In one text God addresses the church as "you worm Jacob." Her attainments are low. Faith is weak. Love is languid. Joy spreads but few feasts. Self-denial has taught but few of her hard lessons. Humility furnishes but a scant robe. Zeal, where is it? She is also sadly divided. Her unity is marred. "Her children have been angry with her." They have been unnatural. Ephraim has envied Judah, and Judah has vexed Ephraim.

2. Another occasion of fear is the apparent inadequacy of the means of the church's defense. Ascension gifts have indeed descended on her pastors and teachers. Still they are not angels but men, men of like passions with others, not vessels used in heaven—but vessels of clay. The cherub in glorious knowledge and the seraph in holy fires—appear not in any of our pulpits. When God vouchsafes his presence, divine ordinances are clothed with a blessed efficacy—but if the Spirit offended by our sins, he withdraws. The 'letter the Gospel' kills—no less than 'the law'. In the hands of the new-creating Spirit it is the power of God; otherwise it is foolishness, a stumbling-block, sounding brass, a tinkling cymbal; and he, who proclaims it, does but beat the air. The weapons of our warfare have no mightiness—but through God.

3. Another occasion of fear to the church is found in the number, haughtiness, cunning, fierceness and cruelty of her foes. Their name is legion. The church dwells like the turtle-dove surrounded by birds of prey. Her enemies present whole empires, and those the most populous, in solid masses of wickedness. Their insolence is diabolical. They shoot out the lip in mocking. They point the finger of scorn. They deride pious grief. They mocked the dying agonies of her Lord. They ridicule her noblest designs, saying, "If a fox goes on it, he shall even break down their stone wall." They exhaust their powers of reproach and ignominy on the saints. They rely on worldly influence. In fury they are like raging waves of the sea, foaming out their thundering menaces. The blood of the faithful they have poured out like water to the dogs of persecution, who have licked it up with greediness. Many a time has persecution

"Sat and planned
Deliberately and with most careful pains,
How to extreme suffering of agony,
The flesh, and blood, and souls of holy men,
Her victims, might be wrought; and when she saw
New tortures, of her laboring fancy born,
She leaped for joy, and made great haste to try
Their force, well pleased to hear a deeper groan."

We may live to see such days. Sober writers on prophecy seem to expect a destructive fury of wicked passions before the blaze of Millenial glory. But whether raging or quiet—the enemies of the church are always cunning. With the venom they have also the deceptiveness of the serpent—that old serpent, who deceives the nations. They lay dark plots. They fill the way to Zion with pits and snares. This is especially true of the teachers of false doctrine. "Insidiousness seems to be a common character of heresy." [Milner.] "Damnable heresies" are always brought in "secretly." If it were possible, false teachers would deceive the very elect!

4. Another occasion for sinful fear in the church is the seeming tardiness of her divine Head in avenging her wrongs and vindicating her cause. Zion forgets that the plans of her King reach from an eternity past to an eternity to come. Forgetting this, the church cries, "O Lord, how long?" "Why then does my suffering continue? Why is my wound so incurable? Your help seems as uncertain as a seasonal brook. It is like a spring that has gone dry." "I look for judgment—but there is none; for salvation—but it is far from me." For ages the church has cried, "How long, O Lord, holy and true, do you not judge and avenge our blood on those who dwell on the earth?" How often is the heart made sick by the deferring of hope. Jonathan Edwards ventured to conjecture that he had seen the dawn of the latter-day glory. Yet he lived to see folly, heresy, fanaticism and persecution mar the glory of that great revival.

II. SUCH FEAR IS WITHOUT GOOD CAUSE.

The language of God to Zion is clear and unmistakable, "Fear not; be not dismayed." God gives reasons, good reasons for such encouragement, "But now, O Israel, the Lord who created you says: Do not be afraid, for I have ransomed you. I have called you by name; you are mine. When you go through deep waters and great trouble, I will be with you. When you go through rivers of difficulty, you will not drown! When you walk through the fire of oppression, you will not be burned up; the flames will not consume you. For I am the Lord, your God, the Holy One of Israel, your Savior." Isaiah 43:1-3.

These words are full of comfort. They point us to God's omnipresence. "I am with you." With his church, God goes through the Red sea, through the wilderness, through Jordan; through the wars of Canaan. He goes with Jeremiah into the mire of the dungeon of Malchiah, with Daniel into the lions' den, with the young Hebrews into the burning fiery furnace, with Stephen through the shower of stones, and with John to the island of Patmos. Nor does he confine his presence to great men, or great occasions. To the whole church in all her states and trials he says, "I will never, no never leave you; I will never, no never, no never forsake you."

In this presence of God there is a blessed concord among the persons of the adorable Trinity. The eternal Father says, "I am with you." The eternal Son says, "Lo, I am with you always—even unto the end of the world." The eternal Spirit by the Son assures us that he will abide with us forever. This presence supposes and implies readiness to hear prayers, to extend aid, to protect, support and deliver. It gives us at hand vast storehouses of infinite perfections from which to draw supplies. Let the church stand on this rock and sing, "God is our refuge and strength—a very present help in trouble!"

Look, too, at the power of God promised to *help*, *uphold* and *strengthen* us. Pious men of all ages have stayed themselves on that almightiness, severed from which the universe would rush headlong into the bottomless abyss of annihilation—but supported by which all worlds travel, "wheeling unshaken through immensity." The Lord thus chides and cheers us at once, "I, even I, am the one who comforts you. So why are you afraid of mere humans, who wither like the grass and disappear? Yet you have forgotten the Lord, your Creator, the one who put the stars in the sky and established the earth. Will you remain in constant dread of human oppression? Will you continue to fear the anger of your enemies from morning till night? Soon all you captives will be released! Imprisonment, starvation, and death will not be your fate! For I am the Lord your God, who stirs up the sea, causing its waves to roar. My name is the Lord Almighty." Isaiah 51:12-15

"Do you not know? Have you not heard? Has it not been told you from the beginning? Have you not understood since the earth was founded? He sits enthroned above the circle of the earth, and its people are like grasshoppers. He stretches out the heavens like a canopy, and spreads them out like a tent to live in. He brings princes to naught and reduces the rulers of this world to nothing. No sooner are they planted, no sooner are they sown, no sooner do they take root in the ground, than he blows on them and they wither, and a whirlwind sweeps them away like chaff. "To whom will you compare me? Or who is my equal?" says the Holy One. Lift your eyes and look to the heavens: Who created all these? He who brings out the starry host one by one, and calls them each by name. Because of his great power and mighty strength, not one of them is missing. Why do you say, O Jacob, and complain, O Israel, "My way is hidden from the Lord; my cause is disregarded by my God"? Do you not know? Have you not heard? The Lord is the everlasting God, the Creator of the ends of the earth. He will not grow tired or weary, and his understanding no one can fathom. He gives strength to the weary and increases the power of the weak." Isaiah 40:21-29

Who dare affirm that anything is too hard for God? He, who humbly relies on the presence and power of God

"is the man whom storms can never make
Meanly complain; nor can a flattering gale
Make him talk proudly—he has no desire
To read his secret fate—yet unconcerned
And calm can meet his unborn destiny
In all its charming or its frightful shapes."

The Bible abounds in exceeding great and precious promises, inwoven into the covenant, which God has made with his chosen, and which has been the joy of the saints in all ages. That covenant is *everlasting.* Time, change, tumult, can never set it aside. Abraham, David, and all the prophets hold their places in heaven by this tenure.

This covenant is also *sure.* There is no flaw in it. It is well ordered. It is the plan of God himself, the work of eternal wisdom.

This covenant is *confirmed* by renewals, by fulfillments, by ordinances, by signs and seals, and by the solemnities of an oath. "God has given us both his promise and his oath. These two things are unchangeable because it is impossible for God to lie. Therefore, we who have fled to him for refuge can take new courage, for we can hold on to his promise with confidence. This confidence is like a strong and trustworthy anchor for our souls. It leads us through the curtain of heaven into God's inner sanctuary." Hebrews 6:18-19.

"No one sets aside even a human covenant that has been ratified, or makes additions to it." How firm then must be the covenant of God! This covenant is *not encumbered* with any causal or meritorious conditions. We are to look and live, to take and eat, to receive Christ and his grace, and be saved forever. No money, no merit is required of us.

This covenant is *ample* in its provisions. It secures the promise of the life that now is, and of that which is to come. It secures bread and water, food and clothing, justification and sanctification, faith, repentance, hope, love, joy, meekness, patience, gentleness, peace, experience, victory and an exceeding and eternal weight of glory. It makes death a blessing. It pronounces the believer heir of all things. It converts ills into mercies.

This covenant is sealed in the blood of the Son of God. "This is the new testament in my blood," says he.

The execution of this covenant is conducted under "the ministry of the Spirit." He gives us the anointing which abides, the unction which teaches all things.

This covenant is never to be *forgotten*. God never forgets it, nor will he let his people forget it.

This covenant is in the hands of a Mediator, Jesus, who is "the Messenger of the covenant," "God's elect, in whom his soul delights," the God-man, the Surety of all his people. The exceeding fitness of our Savior to administer this covenant is often declared in Scripture.

First, "He thought it not robbery to be equal with God." His eternal power and Godhead are never questioned in heaven. As a mediator, he is able to lay his hand upon God.

Secondly, finding those to be redeemed in human nature, he took part of the same. He became bone of our bone, and flesh of our flesh. He assumed our whole nature, its sinfulness excepted. He was tempted in all points like as we are. He carried our sorrows. He shook hands with grief and made affliction his bosom companion. With tastes exquisitely refined and with sensibilities the keenest—he lived and died poor, subsisting chiefly on the charities of a few humble women—he hungered, he thirsted, he toiled, he wept, he prayed, he died. And even in his mysterious agony, he showed his power and grace by saving a thief; and his filial piety and natural affection—by making the most fitting provision for his aged mother. Even after his resurrection he gave many infallible proofs that he was still truly a man.

Thirdly, Christ was pre-eminently prepared for his work by being gloriously anointed by the Holy Spirit. "He received the Spirit without measure." All fullness of grace, and truth, and wisdom dwelt in him.

Fourthly, in consequence of what he was and did and suffered—he is highly exalted. His name is above every name. The universe is held together by him. He summons the stars to fight his battles, and they obey him. His angels at his command confound his foes and save his people. "By him kings reign, and princes decree justice. By him princes rule, and nobles, even all the judges of the earth." Over good and bad angels and men—he sways his scepter. It was he, who struck the oracles dumb. Even his birth sent confusion into the heathen temples. The most famous seat of such worship was at Delphos. When the oracle there was asked why he so seldom gave responses now, the answer was, "There is a Hebrew boy, who is king of the gods, who has commanded me to leave this house, and be gone to hell, and therefore you are to expect no more answers." O yes, the Hebrew boy is the Father of eternity—the Wonderful, Counselor, the mighty God! Devils were subject unto him. Pharaoh, Cyrus, Sennacherib, Herod, Nero—every tyrant and every persecutor did but "accomplish his whole work on Mount Zion."

If convulsions shake heaven and earth, if thrones and empires crumble to dust, if rivers of blood are poured out, if famine and pestilence devastate the land, if "on the earth, nations will be in anguish and perplexity at the roaring and tossing of the sea; if men will faint from terror, apprehensive of what is coming on the world, for the heavenly bodies will be shaken;" still we sing, "O Zion, your God reigns!" "Stand up and lift up your heads, because your redemption is drawing near!"

On the other hand, to his people he is the Prince of peace. To them he is as "the light of the morning, when the sun rises, even a morning without clouds; as the tender grass springing out of the earth by clear shining after rain." You worm Jacob, he *helps* you, he *upholds* you, he *strengthens* you. He makes "the feeble among his saints to be as David, and the house of David to be as God, as the angel of the Lord." "When the poor and needy seek water and there is none, and their tongue fails for thirst—he opens rivers in high places and fountains in the midst of the valleys. He makes the wilderness a pool of water and the dry land springs of water." **His compassions are infinite, his power almighty, his wisdom unerring.**

Before his incarnation he was afflicted in all their affliction, and since his ascension he has once come down within the hearing of men to assure us that he and his people are one, saying to the enraged blasphemer, "Why do you persecute ME?" His church is engraved on the palms of his hands. In the midst of cares and business, the husband may forget the wife of his youth. But the bridegroom of the church has "betrothed her unto him forever, yes he has betrothed her unto him in righteousness, and in judgment and in loving-kindness, and in mercies. He has even betrothed her unto him in faithfulness." And all this provision of mercy, of a covenant with a Surety—was made in mere love and pity—and not by any of our merits. So we may fearlessly reason, If "God spared not his own Son—but delivered him up for us all, how shall he not with him freely give us all things?" Such reasoning is conclusive—unanswerable. It shuts us up to hope. It forbids all harassing *fears*. It brands *dismay* with guilt and infamy.

If these things are so, then every pious man ought to be far more concerned to derive benefit from afflictions, than to get rid of them. We are always guilty when we do not gather the peaceable fruit of righteousness from our chastisements. **From adversity, the church should derive the following benefits—**

1. She should learn the meaning of many portions of Scripture. The Psalms and many of the sacred writings are best studied in the day of darkness, trial, and bereavement. Whatever leads us correctly to understand God's word is useful to us.

2. Trials lead to prayer. How seldom has strong crying with tears ascended to God, except from the hearts of believers borne down with an awful weight of sorrow. At prayer in the whale's belly, Jonah is safer and nearer deliverance than asleep on the ship.

3. In sanctified affliction we acquire increased confidence in God. We find that we are as safe and can be. We should be as quiet when hauled before judges, when loaded with chains and reproaches, when stripped of earthly stays and props—as when abounding in plenty, and having outward peace and prosperity.

4. "The path of duty is the path of safety." Daniel in the lion's den, Paul in carrying his cause to Rome, and Luther in burning the pope's edict—were perfectly safe because they were following the leadings of Providence. God will defend all who work righteousness and trust in Him. A man is not hurt, until his soul is hurt; and his soul is not hurt, until his conscience is defiled; and his conscience is not defiled, until it is polluted with sin. Nothing can harm us, as long as we are followers of that which is good.

5. The triumph of the wicked is short, and all carnal boasting is vain. **The greatest of all victories is that which one obtains over his own evil heart.** "Rejoice not when your enemy falls, and let not your heart be glad when he stumbles—lest the Lord see it, and it displease him, and he turns away his wrath from him." At all times beware of carnal exultation.

6. God will take care of his interests on earth. He will promote the purity and protect the innocence of his church. "All is not lost—which is brought into danger." "In the mount it shall be seen." "Man's extremity—is God's opportunity." "When things get to the

worst—they begin to grow better." "When the bricks are doubled—then comes Moses."

7. Whoever risks anything for the truth, and cause, and people of God, shall ultimately suffer damage in nothing. "He that loses his life shall find it." He who piously leads a life of self-denial—has a continual feast.

8. Let us judge nothing before the time. We are of yesterday and know nothing. Though the Lord causes grief, he will have compassion according to the multitude of his mercies—for he does not afflict willingly nor grieve the children of men.

9. If we see the oppression of the poor, and the violent perverting of judgment and justice in the earth, we should not marvel at the matter. "If you see a poor person being oppressed by the powerful and justice being miscarried throughout the land, don't be surprised!" Ecclesiastes 5:8 . Nor let us be greedy of the things that perish. "He who makes a fortune unjustly is like a partridge that hatches eggs it didn't lay. In the middle of his days his riches will abandon him, so in the end he will be a fool." Jeremiah 17:11

10. All the trials the church undergoes are tests, and show God's people what is in their hearts. So we read of Hezekiah. "When the ambassadors of Babylon's rulers were sent to him to inquire about the miraculous sign that happened in the land, God left him to test him and discover what was in his heart." 2 Chronicles 32:31

11. God so arranges and blesses the trials of his people, as commonly to make them the means of strengthening their love to the church. He, who does not love Zion, does not love her King. He, who does not prefer Jerusalem above his chief joy, is not prepared for glory. Whatever leads us to "walk about Zion, go round about her, tell the towers thereof, mark well her bulwarks, and consider her palaces," is good for us, and refreshes us.

12. Some trials in each age of the church are necessary to keep alive the principles of personal and religious liberty. The world is always cruel and tyrannizing. Every generation of Christians has to fight the battle of freedom of thought, and freedom of worship. The world is always encroaching.

13. Let us often inquire—Why, O Lord, do you contend with us? There is always a cause—a need be—for our afflictions. Blessed is he who knows his calling, his business, his opportunity, and the end God has in view in dealing with him.

14. By the review and remembrance of past trials, let the church gather strength for future conflicts. Often do saints sing—

"When we review our dismal fears

'Tis hard to think they've vanished so;
With God we left our flowing tears,
He makes our joys like rivers flow."

"Zion enjoys her monarch's love,
Secure against a threatening hour;
Nor can her firm foundation move,
Built on his truth, and armed with power."

GOD'S PROVIDENCE OVER NATIONS

"All the peoples of the earth are regarded as nothing. He does as he pleases with the powers of heaven and the peoples of the earth. No one can hold back his hand or say to him—What have you done?" Daniel 4:35

In general men think far too little of God's providence over nations. In great perplexity, when evidently the power of man is wholly inadequate to remove or avert evils—then indeed the godly say—In God alone is our help. If divine interposition is required in anything, surely it is essential in the government of nations. The interests at stake are vast and momentous. Property, liberty, reputation and life, with all the rights and blessings connected with them—are powerfully protected or ruinously destroyed—by political institutions. An invasion of rights respecting any of these, has often called forth the greatest powers of argument and eloquence, even when but *one* man had committed or suffered an injustice. But in the government of nations the rights of thousands, generally of millions, are at stake. If conscious integrity under slander, violence or chains may, from its dark cells—lift up its supplicating eye to the Father of spirits, and hope that he will make bare his arm, and plead its cause, though the person of but one, and he a humble member of society, be involved; can we believe that the destinies of a mighty people associated in a whole country are forgotten before God? If the gentle shepherd, the distressed mariner, the dying prisoner, the orphan boy, or the defenseless widow—may venture to repose confidence in Jehovah; surely may a nation expect that their common and unspeakable interests will not be forgotten before God.

These thoughts derive great force, from the absolute incapacity of nations to protect themselves, or to preserve their own existence. There are but few men in the world possessed of any considerable wisdom in the management of political affairs. The eloquent, the brave, the learned are often wholly unfit for times of trial in the regulation of states and empires. We have the highest authority for saying, "Great men are not always wise." The affairs of nations are so complicated, the interests involved are so conflicting, the passions of men are so turbulent, and a proper passage through difficulties is often so narrow and so intricate, that learning gives no safe precedents, eloquence is powerless in the presence of fierce opposition, courage is as useless as it would be in attacking a tornado, and faithfulness and public services are forgotten, despised or envied.

In such times there is need of wisdom in all the departments of government—a wisdom too that has seldom been attained by mortals. The shrewdest men the world has ever seen, have often felt themselves stymied and sometimes confounded. Moreover, the really wise men in any nation, being a very small minority in fact, are often so in the adoption of measures. They see one after another of the only safe plans, which they recommend, rejected until they despair of success. Their foresight is called fancy; their prudence is esteemed timidity; their moderation is set down to the account of lukewarmness; and their timely courage is called rashness. Every people on earth, at least every *free* people, have at times been like a vessel dismasted, her rudder bands broken, herself driven before the winds, and at the mercy of the waves. **No pilot but One that has omniscience is adequate to stand at the helm and guide her safely through the storm.**

A pure despotism is the simplest form of government in the world. In it the will of one man decides everything. The moment men depart one step towards constitutional freedom, the government becomes complex. The more freedom, the more difficult it is to understand and adjust the balances of the Constitution and the laws under it. Hence the necessity of transcendent wisdom in rulers. **But if great men are not always wise—neither are wise men always honest, unselfish or loyal to their country.** Ahithophel was a traitor. Richelieu was bold, intriguing and fond of war. He destroyed Savoy, Pignerol and Casal. He sent Mary de Medicis, his great benefactress, to end her days in exile. He agitated all surrounding kingdoms with dissensions and insurrections. He had great abilities—but great selfish ambition—and very few virtues. Talleyrand's *wisdom* was the scourge of the nation which he ruled. Pitt was a great statesman—but his wars cost England millions, besides innumerable precious lives, and the loss of more private virtue than the glory of all the kingdoms of the world is worth.

Men who might understand what ought to be done for a nation's good are often vain, cruel and sordidly selfish. When wisdom degenerates into cunning, and political acts are cautiously constructed to secure the elevation of their authors—their very gifts are a curse. Their long and loud professions of love of country deceive none but the unwary. When anyone dares to oppose their nefarious schemes, they cry out, "Are you he that troubles Israel?" They often pander to the sins of the nation. Their appeals are to the worst passions of the human bosom. Their practice is never better than their principles. Sometimes they are drunkards; sometimes they are lewd and profane; sometimes, gamblers or violent. They deride God's name; they despise his Sabbaths; they scorn his worship; they reject his word.

Some have thought that, because in the United States, Christianity has outlived the ten thousand malignant blows aimed at her sacred standard and her standard bearers, by the army of infidels that arose just after the French Revolution, therefore pure religion is here in no danger. But is this not a mistake? In the eyes of a majority of this nation, it is no longer a reproach to be a professed Christian. For years some great men have been courting various religious denominations in order to secure their votes. Hence new dangers threaten both the country and the church of God. Already hypocrisy and phariseeism are by some deemed advantageous in political contests. The world is not without a solemn lesson on this subject. It may not be resolved by any legislature, as once it was by Parliament, that "no person shall be employed but such as the House is satisfied of his real godliness." Yet oftentimes public opinion is more powerful than any statute.

Let ambitious men be once persuaded that an assumption of the Christian's name and garb will advance their interests, and we shall find them flattering the vanity of the silly or superstitious, and desecrating the high functions of their stations to sectarian fanaticism, and putting their hands upon the holy things of a religion, which hurls its most awful anathemas against a *vain show of piety*—and says imperatively to each one, "My son, give me your *heart.*"

Surely then there is need for the insteppings of Jehovah to guide and govern nations; nations generally—and each nation in particular. Truly God is their only hope. If he withdraws his arm—they sink. If he removes his protecting shield—they fall before their enemies. If he take his strong and quieting hand off the hearts of the people—their passions heated as in a furnace burst forth, and *freedom* perishes like stubble before the consuming fire!

It is therefore no less the part of wisdom than of piety, to acknowledge the absolute dependence of every nation upon the all-wise governance and nurturing care of Jehovah for the perpetuity of its blessings. Sober men in every age and country have publicly and privately confessed how the Lord alone did make, and save, and keep them a people. Many a time does the peace of every land hang by a thread—while faction, or violence, or treachery stand ready with their weapons to cut it! Without God's good providence also—nations would soon perish from famine or pestilence.

Very easily can God arm even a *feeble folk* to set at defiance for years together—the skill of the most powerful governments. At one time in this century four of the mightiest nations on earth for years found their arms and prowess held at bay by comparatively contemptible tribes; Russia by the Circassians; England by the Afghans; France by the Algerines; and America by the Seminoles. Each of these powerful states expended millions of money and wasted many precious lives, while God was teaching them that "fastest runner doesn't always win the race, and the strongest warrior doesn't always win the battle. The wise are often poor, and the skillful are not necessarily wealthy. And those who are educated don't always lead successful lives strong." God is Judge of all.

These views are fully sustained by Scripture. If the weakness and wickedness of men show that nations cannot be preserved by human power and wisdom—Scriptural revelation teaches the same. It is not convenient to present all the passages of Holy Writ which establish this truth. The following are some of them. God claims to be the Father and Founder of nations. To Ishmael he said, "I will make of you a nation." To Abraham he said, "I will make of you a strong nation." Very often in the Scriptures does he claim to have founded and preserved the Jewish nation. Again it is said, "He shall judge among the nations," and "The Lord is governor among the nations." God is often said himself—to have scattered nations, to have cast out nations, to have divided to the nations their inheritance, to increase nations, to enlarge them, and to subdue them. Nor is Jehovah burdened with this mighty charge; for all nations are before him as nothing and vanity, a drop of the bucket and the dust of the balance. "When he gives quietness, who then can make trouble? and when he hides his face, who then can behold it? whether it be done against a nation, or against a man only." God has often threatened to punish nations, to be avenged on them, yes, to cast into hell the nations which forget God. These are but a small part of the solemn texts of Scripture on this subject. They are enough to show that **God's providence over nations is**

universal and particular!

They also show that there is cause of fear for every nation on earth. The Lord is their governor and they have rebelled against him. They have been exceedingly ungrateful. What prosperous nation has not waxed fat and kicked against the Lord? How do pride, and vanity, and covetousness, and evil speaking, and profaneness, and drunkenness, and hatred, and contempt of authority, and violence, and blood shedding stain the escutcheon of every nation! How is the permanency of every good government endangered by office seekers!

"Unnumbered suppliants crowd preferment's gate,
Athirst for wealth, and burning to be great;
Delusive fortune hears the incessant call,
They mount, they shine, evaporate and fall.
On every stage the *foes of peace* attend,
Hate dogs their flight, and insult marks their end."

When God afflicts any nation let its inhabitants reverently bow before him and humbly submit to his chastisements.

Let godly men pray and trust in the providence of God. He can deliver them and their nation out of all their troubles. It is his memorial in every generation, that he hears prayer.

Let men praise Jehovah for all his wonderful acts towards their respective nations in days that are past. We have many model Psalms on this subject. It is the Lord who gives salvation unto kings and delivers his servants from the hurtful sword. It is he who makes our sons as plants, grown up in their youth, and our daughters as corner-stones, polished after the similitude of a palace. It is he who makes our garners to be full, affording all manner of store. It is he who makes our sheep bring forth thousands, and ten thousands in our streets. It is he who makes our oxen strong to labor, that gives peace which none can disturb, so that there is no breaking in, nor going out, and no complaining in our streets.

We should guard against becoming violent partisans in political causes. Where the real interests of a country are at stake let godly men risk all except a good conscience in their defense. But let not godly men associate with lewd fellows of the baser sort in their howlings against law and order. "Beware of dogs."

Let God's people be very careful how they participate in a revolution. This may not be done when grievances are few or light, or when there is any milder method of redress, or when it is the favorite measure merely of the lawless and profligate portion of society, or when the good to be gained bears no proportion to the evil to be removed. In such cases it seems to be the duty of the suffering—patiently to submit, humbly using such remonstrance, memorial or petition as is generally permitted. Should these be forbidden, let the pious man carry his case to God. Thus did God's people in Babylon. Daniel, once in great authority there, although a captive, was, under Belshazzar, driven from court. The most venerable man in the kingdom, he was still slighted and forgotten. Wickedness reigned and raged over all the land. The sorrows of the faithful were multiplied. By the prophecies Daniel knew that this state of things could not last long. Yet for the time cruelty triumphed, and he gave himself to fasting and prayer. He and his countrymen seem to have been denied even the right of worship, until the iniquity of the government was full. Then the arm of Omnipotence was made bare. In one night Belshazzar was slain; Cyrus became master of Babylon; the revolution was completed; God's people were bidden to rebuild their city; and Israel were as those who dreamed—so marvelous was their deliverance. The character of the political agitator is anti-christian. A citizen seeking by just means the general welfare and the public good—is eminently commendable.

Let not godly men be overmuch distressed by the false charge of being seditious and disturbers of the public peace. This slander is old and has often been repeated. Ahab brought the charge against Elijah, 1 Kings 18:17. Haman repeated it against all the Jews, whose only offence was that one man among them, venerable for age, piety and patriotism, would not truckle to a tyrant. Good Jeremiah too, the weeping prophet, the lover of Israel, was charged with treason. One high in authority said, "You are deserting to the Babylonians!" Jer. 37:13. The humble, godly prophet Amos was foully charged with a conspiracy against the king. Amos 7:10. In the days of our Lord, the Jews greatly hated Caesar. Yet when our Savior reproved their abominable secret sins, they said to Pilate, "If you let this man go, you are not Caesar's friend—whoever makes himself a king speaks against Caesar." Of the apostles it was said, "those who have turned the world upside down have come hither also." "These all do contrary to the decrees of Caesar, saying that there is another king, one Jesus."

All these charges were grossly calumnious; but they are repeated against godly people from age to age. The world never understands Christian character. With it gospel humility is baseness, faith in the word of God is fanaticism, firmness is dogged stubborness.

When Pliny the younger, as governor of a distant province, wrote to the Emperor Trajan an account of the Christians, he said, "I asked them if they were Christians; if they confessed, I asked them again, threatening punishment. If they persisted, I commanded them to be executed—for I did not at all doubt but, whatever their confession was, their stubbornness and inflexible obstinacy ought to be punished."

Many refuse to draw any distinction between the ravings of fanaticism, and the purest and most humble piety. There is a great difference between the enlightened, humble, unswerving piety of a true Christian—and the wild, lawless radicalism, which sometimes rises up—not from true piety—but from the bottomless pit, and assumes the garb of piety to screen or to sanctify its abominations! The natural enmity of the human heart against holiness, the envy of wicked men against the righteous, whose brighter lives and higher hopes cast a pall of sadness over their character and destiny, and the solemn testimony which godly men in every age feel compelled to bear against the reigning vices and darling sins of men—sufficiently account for the uniformity and bitterness with which the charge of sedition, conspiracy and disloyalty are made against the best men of every age.

Indeed it is astonishing how true piety has always secured good conduct in subjects and citizens, and made them blessings to the land they inhabited. It was so in Babylon, where the church of God was in cruel bondage. It was so in the Roman empire during those three hundred years when

Persecution walked
The earth, from age to age, and drank the blood
Of saints, with horrid relish drank the blood
Of God's peculiar children—and was drunk;
And in her drunkenness dreamed of doing good.
The supplicating hand of innocence,
That made the tiger mild, and in his wrath
The lion pause—the groans of suffering most
Severe, were taught to her—she laughed at groans—
No music pleased her more; and no repast
So sweet to her as blood of men redeemed
By blood of Christ.

For centuries, had the Christians chosen to retire from the empire, their very absence, as Tertullian says, would have been terrible vengeance to their persecutors. How long and patiently too did the Vaudois and their pious neighbors bless the very lands that persecuted them! So too in England and Scotland the voice of railing and slander poured its utmost cruelty on the heads of the pious Puritans and Covenanters, men of whom the world was not worthy. The greatest historian of England and the greatest novelist of Scotland have laid out their strength to bring into disrepute these godly men, whose memory is blessed. Hume is obliged to confess that these men were preeminent in the cardinal virtues, and that the principles of liberty inwoven in the British Constitution were mainly through their agency and sufferings. And after all Sir Walter Scott's sneers, one cannot but feel that those whom he ridicules will by God be adjudged to have filled their place in church and state far better than the men who caricature their conduct. An eminent writer, a zealous minister of the church of England, says, "Many, no doubt, who obtained an undue ascendancy among the Puritans in the turbulent days of Charles the First, and even before that time, were factious, ambitious hypocrites. But I must think that the tree of liberty, sober and legitimate liberty, *civil* and *religious*, under the shadow of which, we, in the establishment as well as others, repose in peace, and the fruit of which we gather—was planted by the Puritans, and watered, if not by their blood, at least by their tears and sorrows. *Yet it is the modern fashion to feed delightfully on the fruit, and then revile, if not curse, those who planted and watered it!"*

How often have the godliest men been cast out of church establishments, and then charged with the sin of schism. How often have they been fined, imprisoned, hunted like partridges on the mountains, or pursued like beasts in the wilderness, and yet have been complained of as troublesome. They have been driven from home to dwell in caves, they have suffered hunger, and shame, and nakedness, and perils by wild beasts and savage men; and yet when their patience has been worn out, and they have availed themselves of the power given them by providence for their protection and defense; they have been accused and condemned for not loving a government, which gave them no protection, secured to them no immunities—but poured the vials of its wrath with a terrible indiscriminateness on the gray head of ninety years, and on the infant of days; yes, even butchered the unborn babe and crushed existence in embryo!

PROVIDENCE PUNISHES NATIONS FOR THEIR SINS

God's providence is over both persons and nations. In this world retribution to persons is imperfect, for they will be dealt with hereafter. But nations exist here only. Whatever rewards or punishments they receive must be temporal. In thrift, and peace, and honor—they have their reward in this world for their justice, temperance and industry. Here too they are punished for their iniquities.

Sins are national—either by their prevalence among a people, or by being sanctioned by national authority. When the law-making power of a country decrees unrighteousness and frames wickedness by a law; when its executive power is wielded for cruelty, or favoritism; when the judges of a land are corrupt, and justify the guilty and condemn the innocent—then a fearful reckoning is not far off. Likewise, when iniquity abounds in the members of a nation, its punishment is near. The offences, which bring ruin on nations, are pride, luxury, idleness, oppression, extortion, cruelty, covetousness, profaneness, hardness of heart, ingratitude—or any of the sins forbidden in God's word.

But the Scriptures make it very clear that nothing is more offensive to God than the rejection of his Gospel by a people. The 60th chapter of Isaiah contains a prophecy respecting the peaceful and powerful triumph of righteousness, concluding with the declaration that casting off the authority of Christ shall be followed by awful woes, "The nation and kingdom, that will not serve you, shall perish." "The character of nations and men," says Dr. Spring, "is decided by the Gospel. As they fall in with it, or fall out with it—they are saved or lost."

This is a weighty matter. Let us consider it well. These remarks are obviously just—

1. It is of God's mere sovereign kindness that ever the Gospel has been preached, or mercy offered to any people. The glad tidings of salvation are the more gladsome, because we had no title to such a blessing.

2. The sending of the gospel to one nation and not to another

is not owing to the superior merit of the favored people over others. "Not for your sakes do I this, says the Lord, be it known unto you—be you ashamed and confounded for your ways, O house of Israel." Ezek. 36:32. Where is the nation who when they first heard of salvation were not sunk down in many and great sins?

3. The continuance of the gospel among any people is an act of prolonged sovereign goodness. He, who kindly gave, may justly take away. All people have sinned enough to warrant God in withdrawing all his mercies.

4. Great favors impose great obligations. The greater the mercy, the greater the responsibility. The Gospel is the greatest blessing ever bestowed on man. Therefore nothing equally obliges a people to receive the gift with gratitude and to make a right use of it.

Nations reject the Gospel by an avowed and general renunciation of its claims and authority, after being made acquainted with them. In every land some refuse the yoke of Christ. Sometimes many do it secretly. But when the hostility is bold and aversion rises to the point of malignity, and opposition builds up adverse systems, and all this with the clear light shining—that nation has reached an appalling crisis! So it was with the Jews. Paul and Barnabas said to them, "Seeing you put it from you, and judge yourselves unworthy of eternal life, lo, we turn to the Gentiles." Acts 13:46.

Let us carefully look at this matter—

I. Sometimes this rejection is accompanied by anti-christian legislation. Such was one law of the Jewish rulers, that if any should confess Christ he should be put out of the synagogue. Such was much of the legislation of revolutionary France, incorporating into its edicts the very spirit of Voltaire's infidelity.

Sometimes a people go further and cruelly persecute all who oppose their wicked course. Ignorantly yet rashly to shed innocent blood—is a blemish on a human government, or a stigma on a benevolent man. Popular violence roused by some atrocity may rashly and wickedly mete out a too terrible doom. Or a cowardly judge, overawed by popular clamor, may perjure himself, and deliver to death one who hardly deserves scourging. But when in the spirit of Cain or of Nero, a people hunt down, imprison and murder the friends of God's truth, their case becomes fearful beyond expression. In his History of Redemption, Edwards says, "We read in Scripture of scarcely any destruction of nations but that one main reason given for it is, their enmity and injuries against God's church, and doubtless this was one main reason of the destruction of all nations by the flood."

The case is, if possible, yet more alarming when the rancorous zeal of persecutors makes them seek to hinder the spread of saving truth among those who are not joined with them by social or political ties. Thus the cry of the infidels of the last century was, "We must set fire to the four corners of Europe," intending the destruction of all religion. So the Jews not only killed the Lord Jesus and their own prophets, and persecuted the Christians—but they became "contrary to all men," says Paul, "forbidding us to speak to the Gentiles that they might be saved, to fill up their sin always—for the wrath is come upon them to the uttermost." 1 Thes. 2:16. This was the drop that filled their cup of trembling to the full.

II. Men sometimes reject the Gospel by making a hypocritical profession of it. Which of the prophets has not lifted up his voice like a trumpet to warn men against this sin? Jesus Christ, in whose lips the law of kindness sat, yet uttered the most fearful denunciations against hypocrites. For false professions, Ananias and Sapphira fell dead by the awful judgment of God. A hypocritical profession of the Gospel is more offensive than a hypocritical profession under any preceding dispensation, because it is committed against clearer light. The real *cause* of a hypocritical profession of religion is found in the desperate wickedness and deceitfulness of the human heart. But the *occasions* to it are principally two—

First—the legislation of a country, holding out to professors of some peculiar form of religion baits in the way of profit, trust or honor. Carnal men in large numbers will submit to the drudgery of religious rites—rather than forego political preferment. Shaftesbury, Collins and Gibbon, bold infidels as they were, were willing to receive the Lord's Supper in the church of England, rather than be shut out of Parliament.

Secondly—sometimes public sentiment becomes powerful in favor of a religious profession, and in some way makes temporal prosperity dependent on a connection with the church. There is hardly a state where someone sect is not a kind of pet with ungodly men in power. The sect most favored is commonly the one that commands the most votes, or one whose public ministrations are but seldom honored by pungent convictions of sin, or clear conversions to God. Those who preach "Peace! Peace!" are the teachers for the men of this world. "If a liar and deceiver comes and says, 'I will prophesy for you plenty of wine and beer,' he would be just the prophet for this people!" Micah 2:11. This public opinion, perverted, is potent for mischief. It knows no limits. It has no checks as every written law has. It can make hypocrites faster than the apostles made converts. Nor will any true-hearted professor of religion feel the less abhorrence to the adulation offered by cunning men, because it may be directed to his own denomination.

III. A general formality without any practical embracing of Christianity, a readiness to rest upon forms, and rites, and ceremonies—is a great rejection of the Gospel. Outward privilege cannot take the place of inward grace. With formalists, profession is everything, principle is nothing. "A pale cast of thought sicklies over all their religious enterprises and turns all their good purposes awry." Ceremony takes the place of holy living. Fruitfulness gives way to a denominational zeal. The receptacles in the temples of religion are full of anise, mint, rue and cumin; but justice, faith and mercy are stricken from the roll of necessary morals. A staid sobriety and a studied *formality* take the place of genuine solemnity and Christian kindness. A whimpering sentimentality is substituted for a warm-hearted charity. The Gospel is professed but its genius is not understood. Some of its doctrines are taught—but it is never dreamed that they require holiness. Baptismal regeneration supplants the renewal of the Holy Spirit. Men reach the fearful conclusion that religion consists in forms.

Such a community, destitute of fervent love—may soon be filled with fanatics, contemplative and philosophical, or vulgar and boisterous, or fierce and lawless—holding to the bloodiest codes and worst maxims of devils, doing evil that good may come, offended at nothing so much as hesitancy in receiving their wicked dogmas, or resisting their sovereign sway. You might as soon find figs on thistles—as meekness, gentleness, goodness, charity, pity or patience in them. They have the Gospel, without the humility it requires. They hear God's word—but they do it not. They are like the "earth, which drinks in the rain that comes oft upon it, which yet brings forth thorns and briars, and which is rejected, and near unto cursing, whose end is to be burned." Heb. 6:7, 8. To such a people Jesus said, "The kingdom of God shall be taken from you and given to a nation bringing forth the fruits thereof." Matt. 21:43.

Those who thus treat the Gospel bring on themselves incalculable evils. The Scriptures say "they shall perish." This perdition is spiritual and temporal. Their souls perish, and with them their dignity, their good institutions, their outward prosperity. Left to themselves, men "grope for the wall at noon-day." "They sit in darkness, yes, in the region and shadow of death." "Their understanding is darkened, being alienated from the life of God through the ignorance that is in them." "Where no vision is, the people perish."

No principle of moral conduct is sufficiently clear to the natural mind, nor invested with adequate authority—to control the heart and life—if one is left without a revelation from God. And if one rejects the Gospel, nothing can establish its claim to a divine original. Without God's word, reason herself is benighted. The very light that is in men is darkness. They know not God. They know not Jesus Christ. They have not so much as heard whether there is a Holy Spirit. "He who has not Christ—has neither beginning of good, nor shall have end of misery. O blessed Jesus, how much better were it not to be—than to be without you." A soul which has no God, is worse than the new-born babe without a caretaker. The worst spiritual calamities for time and eternity await those, who for their sins are deprived of the Gospel.

But there is a temporal perdition, awaiting a people, who, to their other sins have added the rejection of the Gospel. The language of Scripture is dreadful, "Who has hardened himself against God and prospered?" "The nation and kingdom that will not serve you shall perish." A most heavy vengeance will fall on those who having heard the Gospel, count themselves unworthy of eternal life. So said God to the ancient Jews, "You only of all the families of the earth have I known, therefore will I visit upon you all your iniquities." Amos 3:2. With them the long-suffering of God waited many years—but it did not wait always. The calamities which finally overtook them might be weighed against the miseries of the world for any ten centuries of its existence. Any adequate description of the destruction of their temple and city would be too long for this work. First came Titus with his Roman legions, themselves heathen, proud and fierce, with the Roman eagle, the chosen emblem of prophecy for desolation. A trench was cast about their Jerusalem. Then seditions arose in the city itself, compared by Josephus to wild beasts grown mad, and for lack of food eating their own flesh. Thus the city had fierce heathen foes without, and fiercer domestic foes within. Famine with all its horrors wasted the unhappy people until the human mind can hardly bear the recital. Heaps of slaughtered men and streams of human gore were found around the altar of God. A dreadful pestilence was the natural offspring of these things. In short, every outward calamity with which man is commonly visited fell upon this people from without; while all the intolerable fires of frenzy, envy and malice raged within. This state of things was only diversified by new and deeper scenes of horror, mingled with occasional and delusive hopes, springing up only to be disappointed, until at last the city fell, and the ploughshare of ruin was driven over its walls and through its streets by a soldiery fierce and brutalized by the nature of the long-continued contest between the besiegers and the besieged. Tacitus says 600,000 souls thus miserably perished. Josephus puts the number at 1,100,000. In that day was fulfilled the prophecy of our Savior, "Then shall be great tribulation, such as was not since the beginning of the world to this time, no, nor ever shall be." Matt. 24:21. No man can read Josephus' account of those awful scenes without saying this prophecy was fulfilled.

Following the overthrow of the holy city came a saddening series of calamities to Jews everywhere. Long had they spoken of 'Gentile dogs'; but for centuries, he who killed his neighbor's dog committed as grave an offence as he who killed a Jew. That favored people became a by-word and a hissing.

God also cast off the body of the nation from his saving mercies and left them in their sins, hardened in unbelief. "Behold therefore the goodness and severity of God—on them, which fell, severity; but toward us, goodness, if we continue in his goodness; otherwise we also shall be cut off." Let us not think we may treat the Gospel as we please and yet be safe. The admonition of God to us is, "Be not high-minded but fear—for if God spared not the natural branches, take heed lest he also spare not you." If this reasoning teaches anything, it is that God may abandon and forsake a Gentile people having the Gospel, for far less provocation than led him to deliver the Jews over to destruction. For long generations God showed and expressed peculiar tenderness to the seed of Abraham. Even in their deep revolt from him, God said, "Oh, how can I give you up, Israel? How can I let you go? How can I destroy you like Admah and Zeboiim? My heart is torn within me, and my compassion overflows." Hos. 11:8. Let Gentile churches and nations take timely warning from the awful fall of the Jews.

How instructive too is the history of the seven churches of Asia, addressed in Revelation and warned to beware lest their candlestick be removed. Ephesus, Smyrna, Pergamos, Thyatira, Sardis, Philadelphia and Laodicea stand like seven dreadful beacons having inscribed on them—BEWARE!!! Beware how you slight the Gospel! Beware how you leave your first love! Beware how you embrace the doctrine of Balaam! Beware of that woman Jezebel and her adulteries! Beware how you defile your garments! Beware how you let any man take your crown! Beware how you become neither cold nor hot!

The worst judgments are spiritual judgments. The sorest plagues are plagues of the heart. War, famine and pestilence are God's scourges for the nations generally. But the withholding of the influences of the Spirit, the closing of the day of grace, and the withdrawal of a pure gospel are the plagues reserved for sinners of the deepest dye. They are fearful tokens of God's fiercest displeasure.

REMARKS.

1. Let the people of every land study their national history. Its pages are full of interest. God is in history. Let the people of America be no exception to this call.

2. Let us not trust in man to preserve us. The diviners are often mad, and the seers are blind. **God alone knows enough, and loves enough, and is strong enough to protect any people.**

3. Let us all beware of a morbid excitability of temper. The mock tragedies and violence of our theaters and books, will create a thirst for wickedness, until at last our people will gloat over scenes of carnage.

4. What shall be the future character of the busy millions of America, who already begin to compass sea and land? is one of the questions properly called sublime. Shall they be crude? The sternest virtue may be clad in camel's hair. Shall they be refined? The most debasing vices and the most atrocious crimes have often been arrayed in purple and fine linen. Shall they have but little wealth? God has chosen the poor of this world rich in faith. Shall they be free? Freedom is a blessing worth all it ever cost. Still Joseph in chains was a man, whose presence made others feel "how solemn, goodness is." Daniel in Babylon was as sublime a character, as if he had never left the hills of Judea, and the waters of Siloah. Paul dates several of his epistles from under the throne of Nero.

But when we ask, Shall this nation be virtuous? shall its people know and do the will of God? shall they meekly wear the yoke of Immanuel and welcome the offers of redeeming mercy? we ask the gravest questions. "Blessed is that people, whose God is the Lord." All nations shall call such a land blessed, God himself shall smile upon it, and in every evening and morning hymn shall be sung "The tabernacle of God is with men." When every land shall truly receive Messiah, it shall be said—

"One song employs all nations, and all day—
Worthy the Lamb for he was slain for us.
The dwellers in the vales and on the rocks
Shout to each other, and the mountain tops,
From distant mountains, catch the flying joy,
Until nation after nation taught the strain
Earth rolls the rapturous Hosanna round."

But if any people learn habitually to slight offered mercy, their future course will open an Iliad of calamities, appalling to the stoutest heart. The prophetic roll of such a country's history is written within and without with lamentations, and mourning, and woe.

5. Let each man remember his own awful responsibility to God. The way that nations rise in worth, or sink in ruin, is by the individuals, who compose them—walking humbly with God, or renouncing their portion in Jacob. Aggregated masses are the sum of the good or ill enwoven into the character of their component parts. The union of godly men is right, and it is strength. Let every man rule his own heart. He is the best citizen—who walks most according to the moral law and the example of Christ, and who most fervently implores the blessing of heaven on his people and country.

"Blessed is the nation, whose God is the Lord."

"Righteousness exalts a nation—but sin is a reproach to any people."

6. **People of America! Beware how you trifle with sin, how you make light of God's authority, and revel in iniquity.** In ages long gone by, there flourished on this continent a powerful race of men. In the ruins of their cities and fortifications, we see monuments of their prodigious energy and resources. But they are all passed away. No living man has any knowledge of their rise and fall. After them, came the red man, commonly called the Indian. Two centuries ago there were millions of these people, where now are but thousands. Many powerful tribes have wholly disappeared. Others are rapidly melting away. It looks as if God would make a full end of them. Their nationality has generally perished. And shall the myriads, that now swarm on these shores, follow in the footsteps of these old transgressors, and alike fade away under the desolating power of evil, by the curse of Jehovah, or in deadly strife? O Lord, you know. O Lord, have mercy, and grant to us all unfeigned repentance.

But some are hopeless cases. Nothing moves them. God chastises them—but they make their hearts harder than adamant. He invites them by mingled words of entreaty and of authority—but they pass heedlessly along. A word enters more into a wise man—than seven stripes into them. Though they should be pounded with a pestle in a mortar, their foolishness will not depart from them. In their case we fear the worst. "When they cry, *Peace and safety*—then lo, sudden destruction comes upon them!" Yet no signs of devouring wrath now strike their or our senses. Earthquakes, it is said, are preceded by an unusual stillness in nature. **Hell follows close on uninterrupted carnal security.**

God calls the whole nation to repentance. The voice of mercy is loud and tender and persuasive. Will not all, individually, turn and live? Will you renounce every evil way, and believe in Christ? This year you may die. How can you appear at God's tribunal without a saving interest in Christ? Be persuaded to lay hold on eternal life. If the nation repents, it will be by each man bewailing his sins, believing in Christ, and so fleeing from the wrath to come. "God now commands all men everywhere to repent." Obey, and live.

Then the seventh angel blew his trumpet, and there were loud voices shouting in heaven: "The whole world has now become the Kingdom of our Lord and of his Christ, and he will reign forever and ever." And the twenty-four elders sitting on their thrones before God fell on their faces and worshiped him. And they said, "We give thanks to you, Lord God Almighty, the one who is and who always was, for now you have assumed your great power and have begun to reign! The nations were angry with you, but now the time of your wrath has come. It is time to judge the dead and reward your servants. You will reward your prophets and your holy people, all who fear your name, from the least to the greatest. And you will destroy all who have caused destruction on the earth." Revelation 11:15-18

CPSIA information can be obtained
at www.ICGtesting.com
Printed in the USA
LVHW081119160322
713603LV00018B/321